Mirror, Mirror:

A Reflected Life

A Journey from Brokenness to Renewal

by
Carolyn Ros

MIRROR, MIRROR: A REFLECTED LIFE
Copyright © 2013 by Carolyn Ros
ALL RIGHTS RESERVED

Unless otherwise noted, all scripture references are from the Holy Bible, New International Version (1984), Copyright © 1973, 1978, 1984 by International Bible Society, Colorado Springs, Colorado. References marked NIV are from Holy Bible, New International Version, Copyright © 1973, 1978, 1984, 2011 by Biblica, Inc. References marked NASB are from the *New American Standard Bible*, Copyright © 1960, 1962, 1963, 1968, 1971, 1972, 1973, 1975, 1977, 1995, 1999 by the Lockman Foundation, La Habra, California. References marked KJV are from the Authorized King James Version of the Bible, public domain.

McDougal Publishing is a ministry of The McDougal Foundation, Inc., a Maryland nonprofit corporation dedicated to spreading the Gospel of the Lord Jesus Christ to as many people as possible in the shortest time possible.

Published by:

McDougal Publishing
P.O. Box 3595
Hagerstown, MD 21742-3595

www.mcdougalpublishing.com

ISBN 978-1-58158-156-0

Printed in the United States of America
For Worldwide Distribution

Dedication

To Melinda, my precious sister and fellow traveller, and to all those who join us on the road to spiritual and emotional wholeness.

Acknowledgements

I must thank the many friends and family members who took the time to read the first rough draft. Your insights and comments gave me the "fuel" I needed to carry on.

Over the years, two very special "craftswomen" have used their gifts of being "wordsmiths" to help bring this manuscript to completion. A very special thank you to Christine Terrasson and my daughter Roechama for the many hours of tinkering they put into this manuscript to make it a viable book. Though their contribution is invisible to the reader, the author knows that the book is better for it. She hopes that they do, too.

It is with a sense of deep gratitude that I would like to thank my extended family for cheering me on in the process of writing a book — even long before there were any words on the pages. Thank you for loving me so well.

In closing, a special word of thanks and deep appreciation to McDougal Publishing. You have used your amazing gifts to make these words look and feel like a "real" book.

> *When I was a child,*
> *I used to speak like a child,*
> *think like a child,*
> *reason like a child;*
> *when I became [mature],*
> *I did away with childish things.*
> *For now we see in a mirror dimly,*
> *but then face to face;*
> *now I know in part,*
> *but then I will know fully*
> *just as I also have been fully known.*
> 1 Corinthians 13:11-12 (NASB)

Contents

Foreword by Gerard Kelly 7
Foreword by Sally McClung 9

PART I: KARI'S STORY 11
    Prologue..13
1. Where the Journey Began 15
2. Living Between Cultures 25
3. The Genesis of My "Modeling Career" 32
4. Developing Survival Techniques 40
5. Grounded 47
6. Finding Meaning in Life 54
7. Choices Which Led to Change........................60
8. Going Beyond Borders 68
    Epilogue 71

PART II: POEMS..75
    Daughter of Zion 76
    Image Bearer 86

PART III: MEDITATIONS..89
    The Rooted Life (based on Psalm 1) 91
    The Spirit-Empowered Life (based on Psalm 84) .. 96
    The Focused Life (based on Psalm 27:8)............. 103
    The Transformed Life (based on Psalm 86:11) 106

The Anchored Life (based on Psalm 139:1-18) 108
The Guided Life (based on Psalm 25:3-5, 9, and 12-15) 112
The Wisdom-Filled Life (based on Psalm 111:10) .. 120

PART IV: REFLECTIONS 123
Reflections on Psalm 23 125
Reflections on Habakkuk 3:17-19 127
Reflections on Psalm 42 128
Reflections on Psalm 46 130
Reflections on Psalm 91 132
Reflections on Isaiah 40:27-31 134
Reflections on Psalm 100 135
Reflections on Psalm 84 136
Reflections on Psalm 1 138
Reflections on Isaiah 9:2 and 6 139
Reflections on Isaiah 61:1-3 141
Reflections on Micah 6:8 143
Reflections on Psalm 103:1-5 144
Reflections on John 15:11 145
Reflections on Psalm 27:1-4 146
Reflections on Matthew 28:18-20 148
Reflections on Zephaniah 3:14-17 150
Reflections on Hebrews 12:1-3 151
Reflections on Psalm 96: 1-3 152
Reflections on John 3:16 154

Postscript 157

Foreword by Gerard Kelly

There are a small number of people in my life who seem to me to be possessed of a great secret. Some have discovered how to be successful. Some are rich. Some are so effective in their chosen careers that achievements stick to them like baubles to a Christmas tree. A few — all too few — have discovered how to see God for who He is and to see themselves as He sees them. Given the choice, this is the secret I would die for. It is the secret, I believe, that Carolyn Ros has found. Carolyn's confidence in her faith is infectious, and I have seen its impact on those around her, as she gently urges them to find and trust this God.

This candidly-told autobiography, flowing from the exotic beginnings of a childhood in Japan, reveals just how Carolyn came to this confidence, and how often she wondered if her life might unfold differently. She has been shaped by the way the world has treated her and by her own struggles to come to terms with her heritage and calling. Experiencing many cultures and yet fully belonging to none, she has wrestled with issues of identity and self-image. Here is a woman who has been disappointed with herself, disapproving of herself and dismissive of herself, and has finally found the power to accept herself by tapping into the deepest source of all — the knowledge that she herself has been accepted.

Old Testament scholar Walter Brueggemann has looked extensively into the lives of a much earlier generation of third-culture kids, the Hebrew exiles in Babylon. In danger of losing their identity, the generation exemplified in the story of Daniel had to find ways to hold on to their culture and their God. The key, Brueggemann suggests, is the call to remember who you are by remembering whose you are. It is in discovering who owns you that you realize how loved you are. You are valuable because you are valued. This is the tone of Carolyn's journey. Discovering who she is by re-discovering who she belongs to, she learns to trust in the faithfulness of her Maker. I found the story compelling because I know Carolyn, and I know that every one of these lessons has been hard-won and doggedly held on to.

Woven into her memories, Carolyn presents us with her own reflections on scripture and the powerful truths she has come to treasure through the years. These meditations give depth and texture to her story and will prove invaluable to all those seeking to love themselves more deeply by discovering that God loves them. None of us can truly know that we are beautiful without being told. All too often, we stand before the wrong mirrors, crying out to our peers, to the media, to our culture to tell us "who's the fairest?" But if we will address the question in the right direction, to the One who created and cares for us, we will hear a voice so affirming, so authentic and so true that we cannot but know that we are loved. And if we know that we are loved, we can, perhaps, begin to face the greater challenge: to know that we are lovable. Join Carolyn on her journey from self-doubt to overwhelming love, and learn with her that your Maker is the only mirror you need look to.

Foreword by Sally McClung

Reader, be forewarned: Your life is about to be impacted. It is impossible to read Kari's story and not be spoken to in your heart of hearts. The openness and transparency of her testimony is moving, in and of itself, but the "realness" of what is shared will strike a cord in every one of us. We all look in the mirror and face our own needs and weaknesses. Kari's journey is a potent reminder that we are in good company. We are not alone in needing to deal with our secrets, our pain, and our insecurities.

Carolyn (Kari) walks us through the beauty, the joy, and the pain of life ... but doesn't just leave us there. We're taken further, into biblical truths of how to deal with life's issues. It seems so simple, and yet is so incredibly profound to understand that God has given us the tools to grow from insecurity and pain to wholeness and fulfillment.

Our Father, the One who knows us best, who knows our imperfections and self-doubt, is also the One who loves us most! He longs for us to become who He's created us to be. Carolyn, through her own journey and through the wonderful truths she has learned, takes us full circle on this pathway.

I wish I could put this book into the hands of every young person, especially every young woman. I think it would help them deal early on with the pain we all carry. But I wouldn't stop there. I would love for everyone to read Carolyn's story because there are many of us who are older in life who still need to know the wonderful truths that she has lived out.

Carolyn has discovered that God believes in us. We may struggle with pain and with believing in ourselves, but He is for us. She shows us how to discover this remarkable truth for ourselves. God is calling us forth to His plan and purpose for our life. *Mirror, Mirror ...* will help us get there, as Carolyn shares her life-giving testimony.

Part I

Kari's Story

Prologue

Stories can be powerful and yet can only give a one-dimensional reflection of someone's life. The sights, smells and sounds can merely be alluded to, as a reflection of reality. The unique challenge, when listening to a story, is to use your own imagination to connect the one-dimensional pieces you hear and make them three-dimensional, brimming with life, full of action and color.

Early on in life I developed a fascination of listening to other people's stories. Growing up in Japan, as a child of missionaries, I had many opportunities to hear the most diverse stories, as many story-tellers passed through our home. I loved to imagine the backdrop of their lives, for their word-pictures gave imagery and splashes of color, as they explained how they had come to where they were in life and found significance and meaning to their existence. Often I would try to guess what someone's background was even before I heard what his or her life had been like.

In Kari's case, however, I was not able to get a clear view of the past, as I looked at her now. Instead, I saw before me someone who had an easy laugh and a quick smile. She seemed at peace with herself and the life she was living. It was not a resignation to things she could not change, but, rather, a serenity and composure. This was inviting and made it effortless to strike up a conversation

Mirror, Mirror: A Reflected Life

with her. Her countenance radiated a quiet self-confidence that was not out of place. It looked as if this had always been a part of who she was. As a writer, I was fascinated with what I saw, and I ventured to ask her to share her journey, so as to discover her inner anchor.

"In sharing my story," Kari replied, "you must keep in mind that I will be giving you a sketch of events and circumstances from my perspective. The mirrors that formed me and the reflections that molded me are very different than what influenced others who shared the same experiences with me. You will most likely get another take on things from someone else's point of view."

"Fair enough," I said, as it was her story that I wanted to write down. This, then, is Kari's story.

CHAPTER ONE

Where the Journey Began

My story began long before I was born. My parents had made a career choice which would forever shadow and yet illuminate my life; they had decided to go to Asia as missionaries. This "call" they had received changed somewhat during their years of preparation (during which I was born). They had initially been preparing to go to China, but political forces were already at work in that war-torn country, which would permanently close that opportunity to them. Then a summons was sent out worldwide for missionaries to go to Japan, and it was to this summons that my parents responded.

My parents booked a one-way passage for us — the two of them, my older sister and myself — on a freighter crossing the Pacific Ocean. Basic supplies that were needed to set up a home for us in Japan accompanied us in steamer trunks, crates and barrels. After several weeks at sea, we arrived on the shores of a land with very deep visible scars from the turbulence of the 1940s.

Even now, just thinking about the Japan of my childhood brings a smile to my face. It was and still is a land of paradoxes, a land which leaves its mark on your senses. Traditional Japanese interior decoration is stark in its simplistic beauty. The structure of our homes was made

Mirror, Mirror: A Reflected Life

of bamboo. Then layers of bamboo were interwoven between the beams. This was covered with a mixture of straw and mud and plastered over to provide a very resilient-looking exterior. The advantage of this type of construction was that it gave, or swayed somewhat, during earthquakes and typhoons. The danger, however, was that when a gust of wind made it into the house during a typhoon (via a broken window, for instance), the resulting compression could easily lift the supporting roof and cause the bamboo walls to collapse.

The interior of the house usually consisted of one room with a traditional rice matting floor. In one wall of the room would be an alcove where an elegantly simple vase would be placed with three flowers. The sparse furnishings were said to bring tranquility to the visitor's senses.

In sharp contrast to this sparse interior decoration, spring would bring an explosion outside of powder-pink cherry blossoms lining the river banks, and each year the return of spring was heralded by this visual feast. Signs would be posted at the train stations informing the traveller where the best viewing of the cherry blossoms could be found. Picnics and parties would be held along the riverside to celebrate the return of "new life."

My mouth waters at the memory of the taste of the dark, bitter green tea which is used for Japanese tea ceremonies. I remember clearly how this dark brew is made with deep concentration, each participant quietly sitting on bended knees on the rice mats, waiting for the pottery cup to be passed around.

Japanese food is more than nourishment; it is a work of art. The presentation of the food is just as important as the content of the meal. Beauty is very closely associated

Where the Journey Began

with taste. If something is a "feast for the eyes," then the taste will follow. The soft texture of raw salmon or tuna delicately mounted on a little ball of specially prepared rice won my vote as the all-time favorite food.

As children, we would buy bags of salty, dried squid for a snack during movies. During the O-Bon celebration each August (a Buddhist festival that has been celebrated in Japan for some 500 years), we would buy two sticks with a glob of toffee stuck to the top, which we would work at making soft by mixing the sticks together. Every day, toward evening, the streets around our house would be filled with smells from the little kitchens of the neighborhood. Street vendors would also appear, with skewered chicken roasted over a charcoal burner, or the sweet potato merchant, whose cart had a whistle powered by the steam escaping from his little mobile oven.

Images of steam rising from the rain-soaked ground after a hard June monsoon rain fill my mind. The hot summer humidity still causes a very peculiar mildew to grow on damp objects and, as strange as it may seem, this smell evokes many fond memories. This, however, was not pleasant for my mother, who tried desperately to make sure the wash would dry so that this mold would not grow.

The sounds of post-World War II Japan were not the high-tech zoom of today, but, rather, the clatter of Japanese wooden shoes and the hustle and bustle of the street vendors calling out their wares. Each week the tin-can collector would come by with a big bag slung over one shoulder. He would get our used tin cans, that would later resurface in the shops as children's toys. As kids, we would take our toys apart to see which can had been used to make them;

Mirror, Mirror: A Reflected Life

the produce picture stamped on the can was turned to the inside when the metal was used to make toys.

The rare vehicle that sped by sent up clouds of sediment on the dusty dirt roads. In the early 1950s, cars were not very plentiful, and they had to compete for space with the multitude of bicycles that clogged the roads. White-gloved policemen would direct traffic, completely oblivious to the chaos on the road, but, nevertheless, completely in control of all that was happening. I loved life in Japan.

When we were playing with the children of our neighborhood, Japanese was being spoken a mile a minute, and we quickly learned to keep up. There did not seem to be any difference between the other children and us. One of the things we loved to do was to knot elastic rubber bands together, make a jump rope of them, and show off our agility to each other. We did have some strange childhood games that we played. Two of our favorites were "Famine" and "Orphan," games related to processing the ravages of war, which still surrounded us, even though this was already ten years after the peace-treaty had been signed.

I never felt like a foreigner in Japan and could never understand why Japanese adults would call out that word to us as we walked by. I felt right at home ... until I looked at my reflection in the mud puddles and saw my blond ringlets framing my apple-cheeked face.

Foreign children were a rarity in Japan, and, from a very early age, I remember that cameras were frequently being shoved in front of my face. My Nordic appearance was a novelty in a country where hair color knows little natural variation. The Japanese who owned a camera

Where the Journey Began

pursued my photogenic sister and myself as prized objects.

Personality, however, soon started to play a role in how my sister and I would respond to this endless attention. I remember retreating into myself every time a camera came into view. My immediate response would be to frown. I was embarrassed by the endless stream of attention and would try to figure out how to escape it. As young as I was, something seemed to lodge in my spirit, that I did not want to be noticed or to be different from those around me.

***

Some traumatic events took place during those early years in Japan, and they would have a very deep and lasting impact on my life:

For instance, one evening our family and another missionary family were driving home together from an event. I was only about two years old at the time, but images of that ride remain engraved on my mind. We approached an intersection, and when the light turned green, my dad accelerated and drove ahead. Without warning, there suddenly came a deafening sound of metal objects colliding, shattered glass and screams filling the air. Our car had been hit broadside, and it flipped over and spun around, balancing on the roof and gasoline streamed out over the street.

I remember crawling out of one door, which had been flung open upon impact. I was bruised and terrified, not knowing what had hit us. The miracle of that night was that our spinning, upside-down vehicle came to rest right in front of a little police post. (It seemed like there was one of these little police posts at every major intersection.)

Mirror, Mirror: A Reflected Life

The drunken taxi driver who had run the red light and caused the accident emerged unscathed from his car, shouting, ranting and raving that if we had not been at the intersection at that precise moment, he would have been able to drive through it without any problem. Surprisingly, amid the confusion and hysteria of the moment, the police agreed that it was quite unfortunate that my dad had driven through the intersection at the same moment that the drunken taxi driver was running the red light. Therefore, Dad would have to accept some of the blame, for if he had not been there, there would not have been an accident.

This event and others that followed laid a foundation of paralyzing fear in my heart, and this foundation of fear would become my constant companion for years to come. In time, it turned to terror, fear taken to the next level. It just seemed to my young heart like the world was not a safe place to be.

Not long after this accident, our home was robbed several times. One break-in stands out in my mind, like a slow moving picture: We had all been asleep for some time when we were jostled awake by a severe earthquake. I was terrified and remember crawling into bed with my parents. In the ensuing moments, my dad later recounted to us, he went back to sleep and had a dream that he was back in the States at his father's home in Tacoma, Washington. In the dream, he and his father, my grandfather, were chasing a robber, and just at the point in the dream when the robber was about to be apprehended, Dad woke up to a creaking noise near his side of the bed.

Where the Journey Began

When Dad opened his eyes, he was looking into the face of a robber crawling on his hands and knees next to him. Having been pre-warned by the dream, Dad jumped up and let out a roar like a lion, and the robber, terrified, fled down the stairs and out the escape window (which he had cut open to make his entrance to the house). The next morning my sister and I found a pair of very worn shoes neatly arranged by the back door, where the window had been cut out. In true Japanese style, the robber had removed his shoes before entering the house, and he had left so quickly that he forgot them.

I was lying between my parents that night when Dad suddenly jumped up and turned into a lion before my very eyes, and this image left with me a sense that even the bedroom was not a safe place to be. Was there no place left that I could feel secure and out of harm's way?

Due to the small size of the houses we lived in, my sister and I shared a room for several years with our brother (who was born in Japan). We all slept together in a double bed. I stationed myself in the middle, as I felt that would be the safest spot. Then one night, in the middle of the night, I awoke with a start, convinced that I had heard a shuffling sound in an adjoining room. What I was hearing seemed to me to be like the muffled sound footsteps make when no shoes are worn. At first, I pulled the covers tighter around me, hoping to drown out the sound, not knowing whether to hide or to call out, but the rhythmic sound pattern only increased, and I began to wonder how to escape my cocoon and go for help.

Having listened in on many stories told by guests to our home, I knew that robbers and ninjas could be extremely dangerous. (Ninja and samurai stories were very popular in Japan at the time.) I had stored these "facts" in my small mind, and was now drawing on them for "survival." The intensity of the sound and the resulting paralysis in my body was frightening. I didn't even have the strength to nudge my bed partners. Then, as I agonized and squirmed on my pillow, I suddenly realized that the sound was shifting as well. Whether it was seconds or minutes before the truth dawned on me, I cannot say, but eventually I realized that what I had perceived as footsteps was actually the combination of the swishing sound of my own eyelashes against the pillowcase and the pounding of my own heart in my ears. I was nearly giddy with relief when I understood that we were not under siege, as I had feared, and the next morning I was too embarrassed to tell anyone about my private torment.

***

Months later, during the typhoon season, which faithfully came between August and October each year, a killer storm was said to be heading in from the Pacific directly toward our city (Nagoya). My father was away at a conference in Tokyo at the time, leaving Mom at home with us three kids. When Dad heard about the incoming storm, he tried to make it back to Nagoya by train, but the high winds had already taken down the electrical lines, leaving him stranded halfway home. All travel along the coast was curtailed.

As we listened to the radio all day long, trying to follow the build-up of the typhoon, we had an eerie sense that something dreadful was about to happen. The neighborhood dogs, well known for their ceaseless barking, were now eerily still.

As best we could, we closed and shuttered the windows, and Mom, who had always been a fervent prayer

Where the Journey Began

warrior, was praying out loud and reading Psalm 91 as a tranquil reminder that God was with us to protect us. When the full force of the typhoon winds hit, all communication lines, including the radio, went down. We were therefore unaware of the fact that a tsunami (a tidal wave) had hit the coast, breeching the protective dykes that surrounded our sprawling city. Water was rising throughout the neighborhoods located near the harbor at about eight feet per minute. Since our home was located more inland and at a higher level, we were only aware of howling gusts of wind, which sounded like huge dump trucks driving past at full speed. A paralyzing panic enveloped us.

Pressure from the wind built up around our home, and suddenly there was a sound of shattering glass, and the window of the patio door lay strewn on the floor.

Our courageous mom called to my sister and me to come and help her. She put a blanket over the hole, and we were to stand with our little backs against the door, to prevent the hurricane-force wind from swooping in. We knew enough about how Japanese houses were built to realize that our home could easily collapse. Together with Mom, our sole job that night was to keep the wind at bay. She had already single-handedly rescued the piano, by moving it across the room to escape the rain dripping from holes in the roof where tiles had been blown off by the typhoon winds. I have often looked back to that night and thought that we must have had some angelic help, as our physical prowess was not enough to have kept 150-mile-an-hour winds at bay for four consecutive hours.

Mirror, Mirror: A Reflected Life

The next morning dawned a bright autumn day, and the sunshine illuminated the ravages of the "war zone" that we were living in. Our house stood at a 45-degree angle, but had not collapsed. Our poor rabbits, however, had had a wild ride that night, as their hutch had been flung over the fence and was turned upside down in the middle of the mud-puddle-filled street. Tiles from our roof and the surrounding neighborhood were strewn everywhere. Only later did we realize the extent of the damage, as news reached us that five thousand people had lost their lives when the tsunami broke the dykes around the city.

The unpredictability of nature was a common element that produced fear in Japan. Storms might be predicted, and seismologists could register a tremor as it was taking place, but rarely could they warn us ahead of time of an impending earthquake. We were frequently jolted out of our sleep by tremors, and the unpredictable ground under our feet periodically began to quiver and shake, interrupting our daily routines. I remember the chilling terror that would grip me when I heard the glass rattle before I could actually feel the earth under me buckle. We knew the drill of what to do, but we were also painfully aware that there was really no place to hide once the earth started its dance.

CHAPTER TWO

Living Between Cultures

After a five-year tenure in Japan, my parents had their first home leave to the States. There was a buzz of excitement in the air, as they talked about "going home." For my sister, baby brother and me, Japan was all that we knew, and we could not comprehend what sort of country was on the other side of the ocean that my parents were so excited to see. Traveling by sea was the most economical way to cross the vast Pacific, so again our family boarded a ship. Ticker-tape streamers, bought beforehand, were thrown from the deck to our friends left waving to us on the pier. A brass band was playing marches, waltzes and big band music as the ship slowly eased its way from the berth into open water. There was always a moment of sadness when those tape streamers would snap, as the ship reached a certain distance from the shore. Then those left behind would slowly disappear and become as mere dots on the horizon.

The small freighter we had boarded was an insular floating village for us children and offered many opportunities for adventure to our young, inquisitive minds. A group of us kids soon discovered how to open the porthole windows in the cabin, and one stayed behind in the room while the rest of us ran up to the deck, excited to see our friend hanging out of the porthole over the ocean below. We were doing this when I suddenly felt some strong arms grab me by my waist. I had been balancing on the second railing from the top and a sudden movement of the freighter would have sent me into the bluish-grey water below, had not an observant deckhand saved me.

After more than two weeks at sea, entering Puget Sound and seeing Seattle harbor rising up on the horizon was a welcome sight to behold. Little tugboats helped us navigate to the right berth. After we disembarked and cleared customs I have a mental picture of seeing a rope that separated the arriving visitors from those waiting to greet them. It was quite a shock to see there, waiting to greet us, all sorts of little people who looked exactly like me. Later I learned that they were my cousins.

After several weeks at "home," my sister and I became so homesick for Japan that we reverted back to only speaking Japanese to each other, insisted on sitting on Japanese cushions (used when sitting on the floor), and on eating rice with our chopsticks. We missed Japan so badly that we needed the comfort of fish and rice to carry us back to where we somehow felt we belonged.

During this "home" leave, which lasted all of a year, I learned how to read English. On one occasion I remember that my dad found me hiding behind some boxes. I had read in my little Bible something that touched me so deeply that I was weeping uncontrollably. I had no idea what the deeper implications of the verse meant, but what I had read was this:

For all have sinned and come short of the glory of God.

Living Between Cultures

I look back now and can see that those tears were the first expression of someone searching for God. I did not want to miss seeing Him, but I also didn't really know how to find Him.

***

In good missionary fashion, once we had returned back to Japan, many tent crusades were held, with traveling evangelists coming and challenging the Japanese to give their hearts to the Lord. My sister and I were usually the first ones to respond to these altar calls. This was a time for those who wanted to confess something to come to the front of the room for prayer. There always seemed to be something for which I could repent.

On one particular evening, a rather aggressive evangelist prayed for me. I had come to the front of the church with shaking knees, feeling a sense of guilt and wanting to be prayed for. The evangelist laid his hands on me and began to shake me. After the service I rushed home to the solitude and seeming safety of my bedroom. Fear and panic, which had become my constant companion, surfaced and gripped my young heart, clouding my sense of judgment. As is often the case with children, I took the impressions that I had received and drew my own conclusions.

My conclusion was that religion scared me or, dare I say it, that God scared me. I made a vow not to be a Christian, as I did not want to end up as a single lady missionary in Bolivia. This probably said more about what we had seen of single lady missionaries in Japan at that time, but it was paralyzing fear that led to this frightful decision. What I did not realize at the time was how binding a childhood vow can become. Sadly, by this time, I had already started to build up quite a library of secret vows.

Mirror, Mirror: A Reflected Life

Fortunately, other events took place in my life which helped to underline a positive undercurrent. For instance, I loved helping people. I guess I was one of those rare children who loved to clean up without being asked. I thrived on doing the unexpected for others. The following story gave me a positive reflection of something that God had placed as a gift within me.

***

During this period of my childhood, we lived in a hilly section of Nagoya. The houses were built against the slopes, and a little dirt road ran on the incline against the hill. My siblings and I roamed these hills after school, building forts and pretending that we were mountain goats. We were practicing climbing along the side of the hills (in case we got the opportunity to go to Switzerland one day). During our play, it was not uncommon to see beggars passing by pulling a cart with all of their worldly possessions piled onto it. Generally a dog would be harnessed to the cart, helping to pull the load. It was only the poorest of the poor who shouldered the burden alone.

One afternoon I noticed one of these carts passing by at the bottom of the hill. As was the case with everything new or strange, I did not feel immediately compelled to go get a closer look. I dismissed the occurrence and went on playing. In the course of that week, however, I began to take notice that the same cart passed by at the same time late each afternoon. From my little perch, as a prospective "mountain goat," I had a clear view of the elderly man pulling his rickety cart with all of his might, with one hand holding on to the strap that was flung over his shoulder. He was alone and had no dogs. He was

Living Between Cultures

the poorest beggar I had ever seen, and my heart was broken at the sight of him. After a week of secret observation, I remember feeling that it was not right for me to watch the man without doing something to help him.

Without telling my playmates, I darted home, dashed in through the front door, and kicked off my shoes. (This process was non-negotiable in Japan, but to make it easier for us, our parents allowed us to wear shoes without laces, so the process took only a matter of seconds). I ran to my bedroom, got my piggy-bank from its hiding place, and grabbed the only bill I had, before retracing my steps — all at the speed of light.

I had a pretty good idea where the beggar would be by now, and I sped to catch up to him. Overcoming my timidity was imperative, but I had a sense of urgency that propelled me forward. I ran up to the elderly man and thrust my "offering" into his wrinkled hand. I cannot remember if we exchanged any words or not, but what I do remember was his eyes. They were the kindest eyes I had ever seen. Something in them not only acknowledged the gift, but also the giver, leaving me with an unforgettable impression. This whole encounter took only minutes at the most, and then I sped back up the hill, ran into the house and into my bedroom, before collapsing on my bed in a puddle of tears from all the emotion.

Mom came into my room to see what the commotion was all about, and after she had finally calming me down enough so that I could tell her what had happened, I found that it was difficult to express. I knew that something significant had taken place, but words to explain it were hard to find. In many ways, I felt more blessed to have given than perhaps the recipient felt with what had been given. After I recounted my little adventure, Mom said that she was very proud of me. "Remember," she said, "God keeps the books." This was her favorite expression when it came to God seeing the things that we do to bless others. Even if no one else sees, she assured me, God sees the acts of kindness we engage in to make life more of a blessing for others.

The next day I returned to my observation post. At the very least, I wanted to wave to my newfound friend. But, even though this man and his cart had passed our hill consistently every evening at the same time for many weeks, after I gave him my gift, he was never seen again.

The most poignant thing I carry with me until today about this encounter is the kindness that I saw in the man's eyes. Little did he know that he taught me a valuable lesson: Generosity frees the giver. In my own little sacrificial attempt at giving *"all that I had,"* I learned that it is *"more blessed to give than to receive."*

***

All of the events of our lives form the framework that becomes who we are. It is not only those things that leave a shadow upon our lives that create an indelible impression. There are also many reflections of happy faces and joyful moments that form the backdrop to who we eventually become. I have some very powerful memories of good foundational stones laid in my life by my parents.

Not all missionaries understand the essence of hospitality and the power of welcoming others into their lives. My parents, however, excelled in this gift. My earliest memories include countless moments of sharing meals

Living Between Cultures

with other people, and there was always room at our home for someone to sleep over. Even though we never really had a large house, space was not calculated in available square footage, but according to the room that was made in the heart to include others. Our resources were used to make others feel welcome, loved and accepted. A stranger was a friend you had just met. As children, we were enriched by being allowed to stick around to hear the stories told over dessert and endless cups of coffee.

For a time we were allowed to turn the house into a "hotel," and we were the ones who ran the kitchen for the guests. A down side to this "game" was the fact that our responsibilities also included making sure that the "hotel" was kept clean. That translated into hard work, scrubbing bathrooms and dusting furniture. Even though we had some domestic help in the house, our mother never allowed us to get out of doing chores, as she felt that it was essential that we would know how to properly care for a home.

CHAPTER THREE

The Genesis of My "Modeling Career"

Something important happened when I was eight years old that had a great influence on how I saw myself in life's mirror. My parents were asked if I could be used as a model for some advertising for Yamaha pianos. The Japanese economy was beginning to boom, and sales abroad were linked to advertisements that would speak to the Western audience, hence a little braided blonde-headed piano player to the rescue.

I remember vividly what it felt like to be in the spotlight, with the heat of the lamps on my face. My green taffeta dress was neatly arranged, my socks and shoes placed just so. And then there were the endless pictures, with my smile frozen in place. Inside, I was near to tears, as I hated being the center of attention and was wondering why I had been chosen instead of my sister.

When I was between the ages of ten and twelve, Chicklet gum offered me a two-year contract to do a national advertising campaign for them. Three of us, a Japanese boy, an English boy and myself, formed a curious trio, and our photos were seen in ads in newspapers, on signs in the

The Genesis of My "Modeling Career"

bus, train and metro, and at the local kiosks where concessions were sold.

Rather than enjoy this time in the limelight, I was so timid that I would look the other way each time I saw one of my pictures glaring down at me. I recall feeling shame and embarrassment and inwardly retreating into myself. I felt ugly, and the photos seemed to enforce this perception. My long blonde hair had been pulled back into a ponytail, which emphasized my apple cheeks and gave me what I thought was a boyish appearance. I secretly loathed the photos and hoped that no one would recognize me from them.

These little lies seemed to drown out any other words of affirmation there might have been. My own inner voice was louder to me than anything else that was being spoken. Before long it was not only my photos that were ugly; I began to tell myself that *I* was ugly and nothing to look at. I had started to erect a wall around my heart that would take years of patient hard work to penetrate.

Our life over the coming years in Japan was divided into segments consisting of five-year tenures with a home leave sandwiched in between. By the time the next home leave came around, I was a budding, self-conscious teenager, with mixed emotions about making the arduous journey back to what everyone seemed to think of as the big America (though, for me, it was an unfamiliar world). I had developed a deep-seated longing to belong, to fit in somewhere and not stand out, and I held a vague hope that this trip would help bring my inner storms to a place of rest.

In preparation for our trip, I went to a beauty salon to get my waist-length hair trimmed. I had never been to such

Mirror, Mirror: A Reflected Life

a place before, and this event felt so "American." The Japanese hairdresser, however, had a hard time knowing how to cut my long, fine hair. Asian hair is sturdier in structure than my Nordic hair, and so I emerged, several hours later, with hair cut up to my ears. The hairdresser had only been going to "trim" it, but because of the texture she kept cutting it crooked until there was hardly any left to cut. I was devastated to have lost my pride and glory to the click of the scissors.

Needless to say, arriving in the States as a gangling teenager with dorky-looking hair was an emotional death sentence. I wanted more than anything to fit in and tried desperately to look and act like my peers. I didn't know the protocol or what was expected of me, having grown up outside of reach of the day-to-day American culture. Globalization, as we know it now, had not yet taken place. I tried, within the limits set by my home environment, to look the part, with white lipstick and teased hair. It is good that some styles never made it back into fashion!

During this home leave, Sunday after Sunday, my parents were required to visit their supporting churches, and we children went along, dressed in Japanese silk kimonos and singing Japanese hymns as part of the program. One Sunday, between services, my sister and I were in a church restroom, teasing our hair and applying the deathly white lipstick, when a group of girls walked in. They started their own ritual of teasing their hair, and then one of them turned to us and said, "Missionary kids are not supposed to look nice; why are you fussing over yourselves like that?" We were both mortified. Were we really so different from them? If our attempts at fitting in could be so easily dismissed, where did we belong?

The Genesis of My "Modeling Career"

I had been attending an international school in Nagoya, where the entire student body, from grades 1 through 12, consisted of only sixty students, and now I was enrolled in a middle school of two thousand students just from grades 7 to 9. I was lost — in more ways than one.

In Japan, I had set a standard for myself by always getting straight As. I did what came naturally to me, and that was to study. Now I soon caught on that this was "not done" in American Junior High, and I had to endure the scoffing and jeers of my classmates with each test that I took. My high scholastic achievement was seen as some sort of sickness bordering on "becoming a nerd": the ultimate ostracism for any young American teenager.

The concept of third-culture kids had not yet been recognized at that time. These are kids, like me, who have spent much or all of their growing-up years in at least one culture other than their parents'. While this can be traumatic and painful at times, such children also become adept at combining parts of their nation of birth with elements of the other cultures in which they live, forming, in fact, a third culture. However, I understood nothing of this at that time, and I had, as yet, no idea of the blessing that learning how to be a "bridge builder" between cultures could be. I only knew that somehow I had to survive the extended home leave in order to return to my beloved Japan. My coping mechanism was to retreat into myself and to mind my own business. This, however, was interpreted by other students as me being "snobbish" and "conceited." It was not uncommon for me to cry myself to sleep at night. I didn't know how to span the two worlds that I was now a part of.

During this time, a new dimension of struggle was added to my search to know who I was. I seemed to have

Mirror, Mirror: A Reflected Life

a magnetic attraction to the opposite sex. I was viewed as this "mysterious beauty" that guys wanted to get to know. My parents didn't permit dating, but this added attention felt very satisfying to me. It began to occur to me that by seeking male companionship, I would discover more about myself. The guys seemed to see something in me that I was not aware of. I had a very deeply engrained moral code, but I now began developing a coy, flirtatious attitude. Later on, this would lead to some very complicated situations.

***

When I was 14, we returned to Japan, this time to the city of Kobe. Soon after our arrival there, I was approached by a modeling agency and offered a contract to do advertisements and photo sessions and also to model clothes. My job would not interfere with my schooling, as the filming and photo shoots would be done either on weekends or after school hours.

During my orientation at the agency, I was given lessons in how to walk on a catwalk, position my feet and move my body in such a way as to give the best impression of the clothes that I was modeling. Other advertisements required many hours of posing and patiently wearing a smile ... until it sometimes felt like my cheeks would never move back into place again.

All of the attention this generated was flattering, but in true agency style, the company I worked for was headed up by a woman whom I secretly called the "Dragon Queen" because of her ruthless way of belittling me with constant remarks concerning my size. I was often told that I was "too big" and that I had to watch my weight. The international model who was the rising star of the moment was a British mannequin whose anorexic figure was elevated to the

The Genesis of My "Modeling Career"

standard of measurement for all those who would presume to follow in her footsteps.

The words of this agency head were powerful lies that I believed because they resonated with what I thought about myself. I wanted to belong and be well thought of, and this enabled *Abe-san* (the Dragon Queen) to take a significant place in my life, giving her comments even more power to enter my heart of hearts.

Because I had Scandinavian roots, my physical appearance had matured according to my distinct internal biological clock. The only problem was that this made me at least a head taller and considerably heavier than my Japanese counterparts. This might not necessarily affect others in the same way, but I had such a deep desire not to stand out or be different in any way that this gave me another root of insecurity to plague me.

Looking back at my photos from that period, I was perhaps even slender by Western standards, but I "felt" fat when I compared myself to the Asians around me. I was wearing a size that was petite in the Western world, but it was definitely "matronly" for Japan. So I was desperate not to grow any larger. The Japanese can be rather forthright about talking about you behind your back when they don't think you understand (maybe every culture does this). I did, however, understand the language, and the words that were spoken reminded me that I was seen as "big."

This had nothing to do with reality, nevertheless these words lodged themselves in my heart alongside of my own judgments against myself, and these lies had now become "truths" in my thinking. When any little lie takes hold and replaces the truth, all other words become distorted through the filter of the messages communicated on the inside.

Mirror, Mirror: A Reflected Life

Now I was somehow unable to snap out of this way of thinking or to curb my incessant little inner voice that kept reminding me of my shortcomings.

Like most teenagers in my generation (and maybe all generations since), I experimented with the many different types of diets described in fashion magazines. There was the grapefruit diet, the vinegar diet, the protein diet, the bread diet, the don't-eat-anything-sweet diet and more variations that I have long since forgotten the names of. Nothing seemed to work. I was like a little fly caught in a spider's web. The glossy strings were being woven around me, and I could barely keep my head from being encased as well.

One day my sister's friend came over and told about a new rage that was supposed to produce immediate results. It was kind of tricky, but once you got the hang of it, she said, you could eat everything without any problem and not gain any weight. She herself had used this method and, because she was "drop-dead gorgeous," I decided it was worth trying. I squirmed as she explained how, after each meal, I should insert my fingers down my throat, and the food I had eaten would automatically come back up, and that would be the end of it. Petrified and yet fascinated to see if it would work, I tried it first thing after dinner that evening. Sure enough, the desired results took place. I panicked, however, to think that someone would find out what I had done. From the very first moment of forced vomiting, I felt a sense of shame and guilt. Strangely enough, I also felt like I had been given a key of power and control over my circumstances that would enable me to regulate my weight without others knowing. Whatever happened, I knew that this secret needed to be guarded with my life.

The Genesis of My "Modeling Career"

In my home environment, food played an important role. My mother was an excellent cook, and no one could really refuse her food. She was the queen of hospitality, and meals were seen as an important social event, to which family participation was mandatory. Missing a meal in our house was just not done.

In this climate of being encouraged to eat and wanting to please, but still not wanting to gain weight, I felt that my only choice was to create my own escape route. Once I embarked on this slippery slope of enforced vomiting, it soon became a crippling habit, and I lived with the continual fear of being "found out." Somehow I had to maintain control at all costs. A shroud of secrecy slowly began to blind me to what I was doing. Binging and purging became a regular cycle of my everyday life. It is now hard to believe that I thought at the time that no one noticed.

Through the incessant self-talk in my mind, I was convinced that I was not harming anyone. I had become an expert at cover-up. I secretly prided myself that I had avoided the trap of drinking, smoking, doing drugs and sleeping around with guys, but I was rather clueless to the fact that what had entrapped me was a more fatal level of self-destruction than those other, more outward expressions of teenage rebellion.

I loved my parents but could not talk to them about the deeper currents that had been put into motion within my soul. Because they never seemed to ask me any questions about this part of my life, I thought they didn't know what was happening to me on the inside. Shame and guilt are horrendous taskmasters. As strange as it may sound, death itself seemed preferable to having my "secret" discovered.

CHAPTER FOUR

Developing Survival Techniques

You don't just wake up one morning and decide to adopt an eating disorder as a coping mechanism. With me, it had its roots in early childhood. Early on, there were those small but insidious lies that found a resting place in my timid spirit. My childish coping device of turning inward with my pain, questions, and tormenting thoughts became a breeding ground for despair and judgment toward others.

My mother was overweight, and we had a strong facial resemblance, which everyone commented on. So it seemed to my childlike mind that I was fated to be overweight as well. This led me to make a vow that I would do whatever was within my power, so as not to become what I dreaded.

A little tap dance was taking place inside my head between loving my mom and wanting to please her and yet not wanting to gain weight like she had. I could not admit this to her or even to myself. In many ways I was punishing myself and did not dare to admit that I blamed her size for my problem. Deception shifts the plumb line in life so that it becomes a hopeless chore to gauge what is wrong and what is right. I was surrounded by a group of girlfriends who were also caught up in this same

Developing Survival Techniques

"battlefield" of low self-esteem and self-image. All of us were still too young, immature and insecure to own up to our struggles or talk about our hidden habits.

Scholastically, I still excelled at my studies. I not only wanted to please everyone by getting good grades; I truly did have a hunger to learn. My thirst for knowledge and wanting to find answers in life sent me searching in many directions.

What started as an academic project led me to synchronize Buddhism with my very shaky belief in God. I was studying at a very prestigious international school, which prided itself in its academic prowess and very pragmatic view of life and God. Intellectual pride is something that takes years to acknowledge. It seemed so harmless and natural to want to explore the philosophies and teachings of great sages who had written their own pages in history.

At home, I had learned that there was only one way to God, and that was through His Son, Jesus. From an early age, I understood that life was not neutral and that there was a spiritual dimension that somehow was able to influence our lives. I remembered my own small prayer as a six-year-old child.

However, I was living in a culture where temples and shrines dotted the landscape. It was not uncommon to see little pieces of paper tied to trees at sacred sites. These were prayers of petition to the gods. I remember how curious I was about the little bibs tied around the neck of the fox god statues. These were urgent prayers of concerned parents for their sick babies. God shelves and altars were situated in the corner of the main rooms in the homes of our friends. Small altars with miniature

Mirror, Mirror: A Reflected Life

Buddhas were tucked away as silent observers along the dusty streets of the cities we lived in. In the evening, swarms of wild dogs would feed on the bowls of rice left behind as a sacrifice to these idols.

My fears didn't help anything. The roots of fear that had started to grow when I was so young had by now grown into a full-blown tree. Surrounded by images of war gods, fox gods, the red arches at the entrance of Shinto shrines, Buddhas, goddesses of mercy and many more idols, I constantly lived my life with a feeling of dread.

As I entered my teens, the quest for truth, reality or just the curiosity to prove how open-minded I was, set me on a journey to learn about the deeper secrets of the esoteric culture that I was a part of. I felt that it was too narrow-minded to be so bold as to say that there was "only one way" to find God. It was intellectually more satisfying to feel like I could work hard enough to follow a certain code of behavior and, in this way, obtain a higher good.

Desperation to not lose control was the undercurrent of my life. Slowly but surely, my beliefs and experiences were becoming compartmentalized in my heart.

As part of this quest, my girlfriend and I went up into the mountains surrounding Kyoto, Japan, to stay at the home of the founder of a Buddhist sect. It seemed quite harmless, at the time, to spend a weekend at the temple, immersed in the quaint rituals and prayers. The Spartan accommodations and vegetarian diet only enhanced the mystery of what I was exploring. In submitting myself to this level of spiritual exposure, darkness crept over me, which was initially hardly discernible, but it thrust me even deeper into an abyss of "aloneness." I thought that

Developing Survival Techniques

I could combine the God of my childhood and the gods that I was dabbling with, but it only led me to a deeper level of confusion.

***

A deep hunger for acceptance was a motivating factor that spun me off into various relationships with guys. I was always looking for that illusive fulfillment that a relationship could bring, while at the same time trying to maintain a very strict moral straightjacket.

Seeking affirmation and wanting confirmation of my existence by the opposite sex had become an addictive behavior. I always needed a boyfriend at my side as validation of my worth. If I stayed "appealing," then life was still livable — or so I thought. The games I learned to play in the process led to much emotional baggage. There was one particular date who pushed me nearly to the limits that I had set for myself. This exacerbated the self-loathing that had already been cultivated in my heart, spinning me into a cycle of turning even more rigidly against myself.

At one point, I had lost so much weight that my parents, thinking I had some sort of sickness that could be cured with hospitalization, had me hospitalized. Their goal was to get me to eat properly again. I didn't even bother to eat the food that the hospital staff left me. I knew that I would immediately vomit it up, so I just dumped it into the toilet.

The doctors did tests to see if there was some tropical bug that was causing my weight loss, but no one tried to pry open the lid on my heart to see what was really troubling me. I had not yet come to the point of desperation, to admit that I had a problem and that I was destroying

Mirror, Mirror: A Reflected Life

myself. Forces seemed to be at work within me that I could no longer control. The storm that was brewing was an internal one, and because I had sworn myself to secrecy, I could not talk about it.

My life was such a paradox. On the surface, I excelled academically, was popular and had more boyfriends than I knew what to do with, earned a lot of money through modeling, teaching English and babysitting. Superficially, I was trying to prove to myself that life was manageable, but inwardly, I was a small, insecure, terrified teenager, trying to make sense of all that was swirling around me. As much as I enjoyed the financial freedom that my modeling gave me, I grew to loath the "Dragon Queen." Still, having such a fragile inner life made me very susceptible to the hard-driving pressure to stay within the physical limits she set of weight and size. I was caught up in a trap and did not know how to escape it.

Graduation from high school meant that I would physically have the opportunity to leave Japan and go somewhere else and try again. This was what my class yearbook wrote about me:

> *The best description of Kari is golden: golden hair, golden eyes, golden tan, golden nature. She is filled with a happiness that greets others with a slow understanding smile and a soft "Hi." She also enjoys the intelligence that ranked her high in the class and gained her admission to University. She likes fast, deep discussions, and is continually questioning, yet always receptive to new ideas. Her spare time is taken up with many activities: she is secretary of the girl's athletic*

Developing Survival Techniques

association, manages the basketball team, models quite a bit (You can see her in any number of TV ads). Kari plans to go into social work after her studies, and with her originality and great natural interest in people, she should be extremely successful.

Red and Gray Canadian Academy year book, 1969

***

After graduation from high school, I received a scholarship to study at a university in the States. Because I had already crossed the Pacific a number of times, my parents gave me permission to travel alone, this time on the famous Siberian Railway, through what was then the Soviet Union. My secret plan was to meet a boyfriend from high school in Europe and travel with him through Denmark and into Norway, there to meet my extended family for the first time. This proves that naivete and stupidity can reside in the same person at the same time. I was in over my head and didn't have a clue, and I was going to a part of the world that a 17-year-old was not yet equipped or able to cope with.

I first boarded a small ship traveling from Yokohama, Japan, to Nahodka, Siberia, where I would board the train. The ship was full of intrigue, and I had deep conversations with professors and businessmen traveling for some mysterious and unnamed exploits to the Far Eastern border of the U.S.S.R. I had studied the geography and politics of the region, but I had no idea at the time that I would ever be caught up in the drama that hovered over that part of the world in the late 1960s.

The train was only able to travel for a day and a half, as far as Khabarosk, due to a skirmish along the Sino-Soviet border; then all the passengers were herded onto a plane for an 8-hour flight to Moscow. This was only my second time to fly, but I knew enough to be concerned when the plane took off while the passengers were still walking around the cabin of the aircraft. As they jostled each other for space, it seemed more like being on a crowded bus.

Flying into the bustling metropolis of Moscow sent chills down my spine. This was the height of the Cold War, and I felt incredibly vulnerable traveling in the U.S.S.R. on a United States passport. Moscow represented the antithesis to the world-view I had grown up with, and I saw it as the breeding ground for worldwide revolt and turmoil.

Coming at a season in my life when I was battling my own demons of insecurity and trying to manage them by exerting ever stricter control over myself, especially in the area of food, the diet I was confronted with in the East was enough to drive me into a permanent fast. The Russian cabbage soup, Borsch, and heavy rye pumpernickel bread seemed like food for lumberjacks and pioneers, not for a fashion-conscious model.

From Moscow, I again took a train via Leningrad (now returned to its original name of Saint Petersburg) to Helsinki, Finland, and from Helsinki, a boat, crossing the Baltic Sea, brought me to Lubeck, Germany. There, in a quaint little fishing village, I met up with my boyfriend. He had purchased a motorcycle for the trip. We would cross through Denmark and then on to Norway and the long-awaited reunion with my relatives.

On the first day of travel, however, an accident occurred that would forever stand out in my mind as a watershed moment in my life. I was about to be grounded — literally.

Chapter five

Grounded

While we were traveling along that day, quite unexpectedly the front wheel of the motorcycle hit a curb in the road that was camouflaged under gravel. The impact catapulted me forward over the driver's head, and I landed face first in the gravel. Luckily, the helmet I was wearing absorbed the initial shock of the fall, but it did not have a face visor, so my forehead, cheeks and chin slid over the ground.

I cannot remember if there were seconds, minutes or hours between the impact and the sound of the ambulance siren. What I do remember is that I was powerless to call out to anyone around me. I wanted to stand up and walk away. Instead I was lifted like a limp rag-doll onto the stretcher and slid into the back of the emergency vehicle.

There was a bustle of activity around me, as my vital signs were checked. And, once I was in the hospital, I was rushed to what seemed like an operating theatre. My helmet was removed, and a surgeon gingerly started the excruciating task of removing the gravel from my face, knees and hands.

Both numbness and turbulent thoughts crashed in my mind, as I could only imagine what sort of scars would mar me after this episode. Helpless and completely at the mercy of the medical staff surrounding me, I had no other choice but to endure the redemptive pain that I was undergoing, to ensure that no hidden element of crushed gravel would remain lodged in my skin, to cause further damage down the road.

Then, from a region deep within my spirit, I sensed a voice calling out to me, "Kari, don't throw your life away." What were these strange words that I was hearing? Were the drugs I had received to kill the pain causing me to hallucinate? My mind slowly drifted back over the last few years of my life. They had been full of struggle and turmoil, as I tried desperately to find significance and meaning to my existence. My intellectual dabbling with Zen had left me feeling more entombed in a sense of hopelessness and despair than the state of tranquility it portrayed and promised. This quest had fed my ambitious drive to try to work hard at finding a place of peace in life, but it had not given me the rest that comes through feeling loved and cared for.

The sharp metal probes, used to remove the gravel from my face, sent a horrible sensation through my body. I had always believed the lie that I was not pretty, and now I knew for sure that I would be marred for life.

Despite the pain, those strange words reverberated within me. What did it mean, "Don't throw your life away?" As I lay there, images, impressions and sounds pushed their way to the forefront of my consciousness. In my memory, I could hear the midnight prayers of my parents, as they interceded for me long after I was assumed to be asleep. They were calling out to God to help and protect me. They asked Him to give me hope.

Grounded

Bedtime stories flashed through my mind, stories of a shepherd with a lost lamb on his shoulder, of a prodigal son contemplating what it would take to return to the house of his father.

During my growing-up years, I had slept or drawn my way through so many sermons. There was a certain way that I could sit which gave the impression of me being attentive, while, at the same time, I could use my pen and paper to create my own little world. I knew the language being used by heart, but it had not, as yet, permeated my inner core. There, on the operating table in some forgotten hospital near Copenhagen, words of power and significance now echoed through my being: "Kari, don't throw your life away."

After being discharged from the hospital, my boyfriend and I collected our baggage. At the bottom of my suitcase (I had not yet learned how to travel light, and I still like to be prepared for all of life's eventualities) I found my little Bible. It had been my constant companion since I was young, but I took it with me more as a good-luck charm than as something I read.

Needless to say I was not at home in the Bible and had no idea where to turn for comfort at this very bewildering and painful moment in my life. I knew the Lord's Prayer and Psalm 23, but I had not developed a habit to look to the Bible as a source of comfort or direction. In fact, I felt uncomfortable reading about a God who knew me. What would He say about my hidden secrets? Because I was accusing myself at every turn of the road, I could only imagine that God would do an even more thorough job of condemning me than I was already doing. It frightened me to think that I could not hide from His all-seeing glare (or, at least, that's how I perceived it). It was, therefore, not a natural response to open this little black book, to see if there would be words of affirmation or hope for me there.

My face felt painful and looked like minced meat, and the back of my hands and knees, which had absorbed the weight of my fall, were raw where the skin had been scraped off. I was hurting inside, too, at the deepest possible level. In addition to all of that, I was halfway around the world from my family, and I ached with homesickness. I now asked myself the question: "How in the world did I end up in this mess?" For the first time I realized, with a shock, that I could very easily have been killed.

Why had I survived? What was the meaning of all of this? And what did those strange words mean that I had heard?

For lack of knowing where else to turn, I opened my little Bible and read it randomly. It had been read daily in our home, while I was growing up, but because I did not read it for myself, the words tended to go in one ear and out the other. Now, through swollen eyelids, I read the following words:

> *"For I know the plans that I have for you," declares the LORD, "plans to prosper you and not to harm you, plans to give you a hope and a future. Then you will call upon me and come and pray to me, and I will listen to you. You will seek me and find me when you seek me with all of your heart. I will be found by you," declares the LORD.*   Jeremiah 29:11-14

Those words poured over my spirit and felt like a healing ointment. After contemplating them, one word reverberated in my heart — hope!

Grounded

These words spoke of a future. Did I dare believe it? Could God really have a plan for me? I was trying my utmost to control and plan my own future, which, at this point, wasn't going so well. Did God really have something for me, despite my mistakes? If so, how was I supposed to *"call on"* Him?

I had gone forward in so many church services, as a child, seemingly with no results. What would make this any different? Would God really want to listen to me, when I had been so adept at ignoring Him? Why would He want to listen to such a rebellious child?

Outwardly, I was compliant and passive, but the churning anger in me made me lash out and want to blame a host of circumstances and people for how victimized I felt. How could I seek God with *"all"* my heart when I had practiced so hard to divide my heart into insular compartments in order to cope with life? I, for one, did not know how to seek God with the smallest part of my heart, let alone *all* of it.

At this critical juncture, something did begin to dawn on me. The God, who was revealing Himself to me, in little bits and pieces, had nothing to do with the Buddhist teachings I had been flirting with. I was still "too far away from home" to know how to find my way back, but there was a longing in my soul that was being awakened. Still, I had put circumstances into motion that I had to see through to the end. For several days after the accident, to give my wounds time to begin to heal, my boyfriend and I stayed in Copenhagen, before taking a train the rest of the way to my Aunt Dorothea's home in Norway.

I had heard many stories about my great-aunt and had heard that she was a pillar of faith in our family. She was known to have asked God to let her live to be 100 years old (in order to serve as an intercessor for our whole extended family). God honored this prayer, and she passed away only when she had reached 100 ½ years old).

Despite the generational difference, time and space evaporated when Aunt Dorothea opened the front door to her quaint home, with its white picket fence and ruffled, curtained windows. She enveloped me in her ample arms and nestled me deep in her embrace, accepting in me, the generation I represented. She lavished on me all of the love that she still had for her long-deceased brother, my grandfather.

I had studied some Norwegian, so not all of her conversation fell on deaf ears, but her husband, Uncle Oskar, was fluent enough in English to help me navigate through the basic introductions and further explanations of the family history and beliefs.

Tucked away in a town along an impressive fjord (I was later impressed as I learned that the scenery in that part of Norway was bland by Norwegian standards, and the rest was even grander) I saw a vibrancy of faith that baffled and bewildered me and yet made me feel like I had come "home." I was too caught up in my own brokenness though to rightly appreciate the loving care that was given to my boyfriend and me. I was secretly thankful for the forthrightness of my great-aunt to put us in separate rooms, as I realized I had somehow been "saved" from compromise in this area by others stronger than myself.

I discovered that the delicacies from my childhood were actually everyday fare in this beautiful country of my forefathers. Now the little demons within me battled the small dilemma of how to enjoy the food without overindulging. I had not yet learned how to answer this perplexing question. My response was to go with the crowd and punish myself later. I did not even have to think about retaining the food. My body was so deeply in the clutch of this destructive habit that it was a natural response every time I ate to expel the food. The shroud of guilt and shame was tucked around me like a secretive cloak. No one, absolutely no one, must know what was going on after each meal.

The nature of deception is that you cannot imagine that anyone else knows what is happening inside of you. I was very athletic and a star at keeping up appearances. I did not think that anyone would guess at the duplicity that was going on under my veneer of composure. The truth is that anyone with even a little discernment can detect the telltale signs of an eating disorder. How could I stay so slender if I consumed as much as I did? And then, at night, the words I had heard would return to haunt me: "Kari, don't throw your life away."

CHAPTER SIX

Finding Meaning in Life

After my trip through Europe, I was finally brought back to where my initial journey had started 18 years before. The university I had chosen to attend was in the city of my birth, Seattle, Washington. Of all of the places I had been on earth, somehow it seemed like I had some sort of roots there.

My boyfriend was in his final year of university on the East Coast of the US, leaving us only our vacation times to see each other. In the days before email or Facebook, this meant that our "daily conversations" together entailed writing endless letters back and forth to each other.

One summer, we both worked as part of the crew on a sailboat, sailing between Maine and Nova Scotia. That month-and-a-half adventure was loaded with thrills and excitement, as the radio broke down during an extensive period of fog, leaving us very vulnerable, when sailing through the major shipping lanes, with large ships on either side of us. I was the cook for the crew, but also had to sail the boat when we were short-handed. The trip took a turn for the worse when we got caught in a storm and the mast broke off, leaving us stranded in the Atlantic. The US Coastguard eventually "found" us and brought us to safety.

Finding Meaning in Life

At university, outwardly, I was a slender, shy, cute freshman. Inwardly, I was battling the questions of meaning, significance, belonging, beauty, suffering and death. I had seen the world in its exaggerated contrasts of East and West, with ideologies that clashed (communism and capitalism, poverty and plenty). My deepest questions had not yet been answered. I wanted to know why I was here on earth. I wanted to know what my worth was or would I only be judged by my exterior?

My motorcycle injuries had healed miraculously without leaving facial scarring, and the facial wounds eventually healed without leaving the deep wrinkles and scarring that I still had on the back of my hands and knees. I was overjoyed when my facial skin began to get smooth again, and I was able to avoid the endless questions others were asking about my accident. The wounds and scarring on my soul, however, took years to heal. At intervals, the words that I had heard while lying on the operating table in Copenhagen returned to challenge my heart: "Kari, don't throw your life away." I was at a loss to know what those words really meant or how I could change the direction my life was heading.

***

Courage knows many faces, but there is a type of courage that is not readily seen or acknowledged. It is when someone gets up enough nerve to talk to an MK (missionary kid), who supposedly "knows it all," and explains to them in common language that they need to repent and turn their life over to God. A fellow university student had that kind of courage and sat me down across from him at a table in the cafeteria one day and said, "Kari, you are a sinner, just like everyone else. God doesn't have any grandchildren. Even though you have grown up in church and have been a part of a missionary family, God still is saying to you that you need to repent and confess your sins and ask Jesus to be number one in your life."

From the deep recesses of my memory, the picture of a small child surfaced. Her little apple cheeks were covered with tears, and her ringlets were bouncing up and down with the heavy sobs. Her heart-wrenching cry was a result of her reading a short verse: *"For all have sinned and come short of the glory of God."* I remembered my prayer from so long ago of not wanting to come short or miss seeing God's glory. My life had taken so many strange turns that it was hard to believe that I had once been that girl hiding behind those boxes using my newly acquired skill to read such profound words.

While the student was explaining how to repent, another memory wrestled itself to the forefront of my mind. Those haunting words that I had heard while in the hospital resonated through my heart. Instead of throwing my life away, I realized that I could give it away to God. The confusion and fog that had clouded my mind for so long began to lift. It was as if I was beginning to understand that the answers I was seeking for had to do with the verse that I had randomly read several months earlier. I was being given an invitation to a new life, to a new beginning, to a new future. Could God really love this confused, yet courageous, 18-year-old who had been secretly battling her own demons? I wanted so desperately to change, but knew that I was powerless to do it on my own. I had tried so often in the past, making promises to myself, punishing myself when I couldn't achieve the elusive goal of deliverance from my destructive habit. Could God really love me as I was right then, or did I somehow have to change first?

***

Finding Meaning in Life

The shroud of self-loathing and self-hatred are irrational chains that bind the victim with greater and greater force. They are anchored in lies that grow with time. All that is negative seems to attach itself onto each link, making the way back to "normal" life seemingly more hopeless with each ensuing day.

The key to the lock on this chain was given to me when my friend said, "Kari, confess that you cannot do it on your own. You can ask God for His help. He has already paid the price for you to be free. You know that you cannot make it solely on your own willpower. You have tried to change, and it hasn't worked. Ask Him to come and change you. He is offering His forgiveness. He will also enable you to forgive yourself."

***

Forgive myself? Was that even possible? More than anything else, I wanted to be free from that which had enslaved me and all that it meant in my life. I had never dared call it by name, as it felt like it was a part of someone else's life. I was living in such denial that I could not admit to myself that I had a problem, and I felt that my life would truly end if I admitted that I needed help. And yet … I was now being offered a key. With faltering words and a small, whimpering voice, I asked God for help. I confessed that I had tried to make it on my own, and I asked Him to forgive me of my sins.

I was well aware of the fact that I had missed the mark. It was hard to confess my own brokenness, but I had (finally) come to a point of desperation that I wanted God to meet me where I was. And that is exactly what happened. For the first time, my spirit felt bathed with a sense of relief. I actually felt forgiven, and a spark of hope was ignited within me.

One of the first changes I noticed was that I had a desire to read the Bible. I didn't understand all that I was reading, but I knew there was life in the words that I was consuming. I read about being a *"new creation"* and that the old had gone, and the new had come. I still had not verbalized the crippling habit that had handicapped me for four years. I half expected to wake up the next morning and to have everything different … no binging, purging or self-destructive thoughts. I had yet to learn that there is a process called *"the renewing of your mind."*

The more I read the Bible, however, the more I was confronted with an alarming thought: *"The word of God is living and active. Sharper than any double-edged sword, it penetrates even to dividing soul and spirit, joints and marrow; it judges the thoughts and attitudes of the heart. Nothing in all creation is hidden from God's sight. Everything is uncovered and laid bare before the eyes of him to whom we must give account"* (Hebrews 4:12-13). Somehow, my conduct seemed incredibly inadequate. Who was I trying to hide from? If God could see me (and His Word says that He can), who was I fooling?

This was a rude awakening. It brought a level of desperation into my spirit, which increased the urgency to change my habits. I knew enough to realize that this self-destructive behavior was not pleasing to God, nor did it have a place in the life of one who had become a *"new creation."* By sheer will power, I began to change the compulsive habits that had so ruled my life, for I had not yet learned that I could ask God to help me through the power of His Holy Spirit. The peaks and valleys began to change, and I relegated this shameful season of my life to the dungeon of my soul.

I still carried a deep level of shame, as a result of the motorcycle accident. The outward scars had healed, but the scar on my soul left me believing that I had been marred for life.

Finding Meaning in Life

I never shared with my new friends at university that I had been a model, as I was afraid that they would scoff in disbelief. I decided that I would completely cut myself off from my recent history. There were so many complicated sides to my life. I had been "forgiven," and this was what I decided to wrap around myself, hoping in this way to avoid looking at the deeper issues that had gone into me becoming who I was.

The whole concept of "grace" was still very illusive. "To receive what I didn't deserve" was okay, in theory, and definitely okay for someone else, but I wanted to work for it, earn it, and perform to get it, anything to hear that I had done my best to deserve what I got. Having driven myself, from the moment that I had learned how to read, to be a straight-A student, it was incomprehensible to think that I could just sit back and receive without any major effort on my part.

***

While I was at a student retreat at university, another dramatic change came to my life. During that weekend I learned more about the empowering of the Holy Spirit, who could enable me to live my life as God had intended me to live it. This was the first step to dismantling the inner fortress that I was still living in.

A new level of joy and freedom, that I had never experienced before, began to flood my spirit. If this was what true freedom felt like, I surely wanted more of it. I took my next baby steps to ask God to really set me free. I did not know that this new experience would be tested the last day of the retreat.

CHAPTER SEVEN

Choices Which Led to Change

That night, when I got home, my boyfriend called long distance for a chat. Being so far apart was hard for us, and it was very expensive to call in those days, making each "phone date" we had something very special. That night, when he called, I was bubbling over with excitement and trying to find the right words to describe to him what I had experienced and the fact that something major was changing inside of me. We had been through so much together, and now I wanted him to know all about this change that was taking place in my heart.

It is difficult to recollect, after so many years, exactly how the conversation shifted as dramatically as it did, but I can never forget his answer. In a quiet tone, he said, "Kari, I've had enough. You have to choose between God or me. You can't have us both."

I was perplexed and confounded to know how to answer. We had shared such experiences as the accident in Denmark and our travels through Europe. We had also worked together as crew on that boat sailing between Maine and Nova Scotia, as a summer job, and we had been planning to spend the rest of our lives together. Now this.

Before that weekend, I definitely would have chosen the tangible fact of my present relationship above a relationship with God, but now I had experienced a sparkle of hope, a whiff of freedom, a peek behind the scenes of a life that truly was new. I couldn't put another person above God. It wouldn't be fair to even imagine that *anyone* would be able to take the place of the One who was offering to make me whole.

With halting voice, because the choice was difficult and painful, I answered him, "I choose God." Had I really lost my mind? Was I ready to let go of someone I had loved for years for Someone who I was just beginning to know? That night, as I lay on my bed, my body was wracked with deep sobs. Letting go and letting God meet me was a new experience. Dare I trust God with not only my broken past, my broken heart, but now, also with my seemingly broken future?

An unusual thing happened as I lay there. A deep peace came over me. It was weird and incomprehensible, yet there was a sense that this was probably not the end of the world, but rather the beginning of something new and wonderful. The words echoed again in my heart: "Kari, don't throw your life away." And now a new element was added to the message: "I have plans to prosper you and not to harm you, plans to give you a hope and a future."

***

Enduring change does not happen overnight. There are moments of grace that can speed up the process, but the level of heart transformation that results in a changed lifestyle takes time. Over the ensuing years, I learned to take baby steps of faith. It was not even easy for my family to notice the change that I felt was happening within me.

Mirror, Mirror: A Reflected Life

We know each other within a context of family, and it is harder to live a changed life among those who have known us from before. We tend to know which buttons to push or avoid in the interactions with each other. This does not always bring out the best. Time is needed to allow new patterns to develop within us ... and also within our relationships.

***

As my studies and time progressed, a desire grew in my heart to learn more about the Bible. As I noted earlier, from my earliest childhood, I had either dozed through or drawn pictures during many church services, but now I had come to the place of wanting to know more for myself and wanting to put myself in a situation to be taught.

Although I had diligently put a lid on my past, I still had recurring bouts of fear — irrational, terrifying fear. As noted in the early chapters, this fear had its breeding ground in various traumas from my childhood, but it also included different people whom I had interacted with during my growing-up years. A vivid memory surfaced from years gone by regarding fear and how deeply this had been established in my heart.

***

As a teenager, I had lived with my family in a neighborhood of Kobe where the Japanese mafia, called the Yakuza, had their headquarters. The clan's family name was the Yamaguchigun. It was easy to pick out the members of this gang in a crowd, as they had a certain standardized outfit they wore. They were generally immaculately dressed, with hip-hugging, bell-bottom slacks, an alligator skin belt, nice leather shoes, topped off with a neatly pressed open-collared shirt. Their hair

Choices Which Led to Change

was buzzed into a crewcut or slicked back in an "Elvis" style pompadour.

The Yakuza is a criminal organization that accrues its wealth through extortion, gambling, racketeering and other such practices. The tight-knit clan is known for its feudal loyalty to the godfather, whose position is filled with both myth and legend. Each member can make amends for a "failure" by having the little pinkie on their left hand chopped off and presented to the "godfather." Their tattoos are exceptional in their subject matter and often cover the entire body.

I had heard enough stories of the ruthlessness of this group to let me know that I had to keep a safe distance from them, but just their presence in the same city sent chills up and down my spine. As much as I loved Japan, this reality gave me a permanent sense of insecurity. This was a lurking fear that I was not able to shake off.

***

I decided to return to Europe for my quest of learning more about God and enrolled in Bible college there. During my time at Bible college, one of my teachers gave me some very helpful advice: "Kari, go look up in a concordance every verse you can find in the Bible on the subject of fear. Spend some time meditating on what you read, and ask the Holy Spirit to set you free from those things that you dread." This advice gave me an anchor. I had felt like a little boat being overwhelmed by the bigness of the waves. It had found a safe harbor, but I was still being battered around, as the mooring had not yet been firmly applied. In Hebrews 2:14-15, the writer speaks about the amazing work of the cross: *"That through death He might render powerless him who had the power of death, that is, the devil, and might free those who through fear of death were subject to slavery all their lives"* (NASB). The veil over my eyes was beginning to lift.

At the root of my fear was the fear of death. The Lord was speaking to me through these verses that He had conquered Satan and that He wanted to set me free from the bondage and slavery that I had been under. Very timidly I went back to the teacher and asked her to pray with me, as I didn't really know how to do it for myself. She led me through a prayer of deliverance and encouraged me to renounce the things of darkness that I had opened my heart to. Almost immediately, I could feel the choking chain of fear loosing its grip. I was learning a very valuable lesson: prayer united with faith is a powerful weapon.

I went on to read: *"For God has not given us a spirit of timidity, but of power and love and discipline"* (2 Timothy 1:7, NASB). In another cross-reference it says that we have not received *"a spirit of slavery leading to fear again."* The power and truth of these words became my own prayer and declaration. Because of the blood of Jesus, I was no longer a slave to fear, anxiety, timidity and death. Lightness crept into my spirit, as I began to grasp the freedom that I was being offered.

***

Years later, when I moved back to live in Japan for several years, to work as a newly-wed (my husband and I had met during my Bible school training), I had a very strong *déjà vu* moment. About a month into our marriage, I began to have horrifying nightmares. It felt like a choking darkness would sweep over me while I slept,

Choices Which Led to Change

paralyzing me so that I could not even call out to my husband for help. Before going to sleep, we would pray and read a psalm or two, but the nightmare continued, recurring over several evenings.

One night I woke up in a cold sweat. It felt like an evil presence was trying to grab hold of me. I remember calling out to Jesus and saying: "I belong to You, Jesus. You paid the price for my life. I submit only to Your Lordship, and the darkness must leave, in Jesus' name." I fell back to sleep, only to have a very amazing dream. In my dream, I felt the hot breath of darkness try to come over me and reclaim me. Then, just before I was grabbed, a very shining being stood up between my attacker and myself and said: "She is mine! Be gone!"

***

The depth of this delivering power was underlined years later when I was once again back in Japan for a week of teaching and found myself confronted with some of these memories. It was a year after the Kobe earthquake of 1995, and I had been invited to be part of a memorial service that the local churches were hosting. After the service, there was going to be a procession, called the March for Jesus, through the streets of Kobe.

Even a year after the quake, devastation was everywhere. The port city had been destroyed, and shock waves from it had reverberated throughout the world, as the stock market plummeted. Physically, the scars of those few violent minutes would take years to repair.

During the memorial service, speeches were given and prayers were prayed. Then the group of several hundred believers started to sing (in Japanese) a song I knew well in English. It was Bill Gaither's *Because He Lives*:

Mirror, Mirror: A Reflected Life

Because He lives, I can face tomorrow,
Because He lives, all fear is gone,
Because I know He holds the future,
And life is worth the living, just because He lives.

With deep conviction, I joined in and sang from the bottom of my heart. There will never be a time when earthquakes or typhoons will cease to come. They are just part of the world as we know it. Grief and sorrow are real companions when family and friends die and worldly possessions are crushed beyond salvaging. Yet it is possible to have peace in the midst of these storms. This is not resignation to a fatalistic death wish, but courage to face the future based on the reality that God is there!

But the revelation of the depth of God's miraculous deliverance was not over yet. After the service, the crowd moved in a very orderly, Japanese fashion, onto the streets. I couldn't contain my emotions upon seeing this group boldly proclaiming their faith in the Creator God who had given His Son so that they could have life. I don't know which is harder to believe, that the Japanese Christians were singing praises while we were walking out in public on the streets, or that I had joined them. In that moment I knew first-hand what it meant to be truly set free from the shackles of tormenting fear. In joining with the group, I was making a public statement that I was in agreement with what they represented.

As the procession continued, my attention was slowly drawn to the person I just happened to be walking next to. One of his hands was raised in the air, and I noticed immediately that he was missing the little finger on his left hand. There were telltale signs of tattoos, inching

Choices Which Led to Change

their way down his arm, as his shirtsleeve moved with his waving motion. He was calling out to the onlookers and saying, "You can see that I have been with the Yakuza. You must know all of the horrific things that I am guilty of ... , but I tell you today ... , I know that my sins have been forgiven because of what Jesus has done for me on the cross. It is possible to have a new beginning. I am living proof, because my debt has been paid."

Tears of incredible joy filled my eyes. The haunting terror and fear that I had known regarding the Yakuza had imprisoned me, but now I had the honor of walking next to someone whom I had been terrified of while I was growing up. Both of us were the same now. We had both received forgiveness and grace. Nothing of his past or mine would have qualified us to walk together in such a procession, but what united our hearts was that we had been given a second chance at life because of the redeeming work of Jesus Christ — nothing more and nothing less.

CHAPTER EIGHT

Going Beyond Borders

After teaching in Japan for two years, my husband and I moved to his home country, the Netherlands. For the first ten years there we worked with teenagers and young adults in both a rehab setting and as youth pastors.

During that time, I met many who were crippled in their lives due to the habits and addictions that were tormenting them. I knew the language of deliverance and how to come to the cross to receive forgiveness and new life, but a part of my own past was still buried in a very deep place, and I was not yet able to look at it. Shame and guilt had a hold on me and had silenced me. I didn't dare believe that a day would ever come when I could look at my own brokenness and know that the issues had been dealt with completely and that I had been healed enough to talk with others about what I had been through.

***

We were now on staff at a church, and, as part of the Christmas celebration, we had a time of prayer and sharing communion together. In preparation for this, we were to share with the person sitting next to us (other than our spouse). I turned to my colleague, and out of the blue, he said to me, "Kari, you still need a lot of inner healing." In my heart of hearts, I knew that the Lord was

Going Beyond Borders

saying, "Now is the time for the lid to come off of your past. Look at it, acknowledge the hurt, pain, resentment, judgment and vows that you have made against yourself and others. There is another level of repentance to go to, and you will be healed when you do it."

It had become my custom to ask the Lord to give me something from His Word as a confirmation of what He was saying. Later, in my readings, I came to Zephaniah 3:14-17:

> *Sing, O Daughter of Zion; shout aloud, O Israel! Be glad and rejoice with all your heart, O Daughter of Jerusalem! The LORD has taken away your punishment, he has turned back your enemy. The LORD, the King of Israel, is with you; never again will you fear any harm. On that day they will say to Jerusalem, "Do not fear, O Zion; do not let your hands hang limp. The LORD your God is with you, he is mighty to save. He will take great delight in you, he will quiet you with his love, he will rejoice over you with singing."*

I realized that I'd had trouble believing that God could truly and unconditionally love me. By facing my past, owning up to my wrong choices, asking God for forgiveness and extending forgiveness to those who had hurt me in the past, it would no longer have the power to haunt me. I did not need to live in dread or fear that someone would discover my "deep dark secret" of the eating disorder I'd had. Jesus knew, and I knew. I had to take responsibility for my choices and ask for forgiveness and healing.

***

Mirror, Mirror: A Reflected Life

The journey toward wholeness is not a matter of shifting blame and trying to figure out who did what to whom. It starts by owning up to the brokenness that has been woven into the fabric of your life. Others, either knowingly or unwittingly, had inflicted some of the injuries that I experienced. But some of them were also self-inflicted, because of the lies I had embraced.

***

Trusted friends were needed along the journey. As I prayed out prayers of confession, their eyes mirrored the forgiveness and acceptance the Father had for me. Now my heart has learned how to sing, as I know that I am loved. Even though there are stains from the past, the One from whose heart all blessings flow has encompassed me with His redeeming love. I do not need to fear disaster any longer. I can even look into the mirror and see His reflection of love through my eyes, not only for others, but also for myself.

Epilogue

As a writer, in recounting Kari's story, I have had to learn how to live with the tension of some unanswerable questions. Could I, as Kari in her past, have avoided the damaging things that I've been through? In my growing-up years, I was surrounded by the teachings of the Bible. As regularly as I took my vitamins, truth was spoken out daily in my hearing. What caused the lies to take root and wreak such havoc during my formative years?

There are those who say that you must identify those persons who are to blame for mistakes of the past in order to be set free. I have discovered that identifying principle people in my life who have shaped and formed me, but also who have wounded and hurt me, has been beneficial, when I could come to the place of extending forgiveness and of receiving forgiveness in return. Extending forgiveness is a process of releasing the other person, problem, or pain into the hands of Jesus. It does not always mean that I will have the opportunity to physically ask the other person for forgiveness or extend forgiveness to them, but no one can keep me from forgiving. The reality is that I live my life before the audience of One. The question, at the end of time, will be: what did I do with His grace and forgiveness that He is offering me?

Mirror, Mirror: A Reflected Life

In my case, the prison walls were made thicker each year that the denial, guilt, and shame were left unchecked. The deepest hunger of my life for acceptance, meaning, and significance was left unsatisfied, as I had no greater source that I could draw from than myself. Approval, recognition, and affirmation were yearned for, but remained elusive. All the while, my deliverance was only a prayer away.

For those who are reading this story and are struggling with food addictions, take the time to do some additional reading. An eating disorder is not just a passing rage or fashion statement but, rather, a destructive pattern that will leave long-term physical damage, if left unchecked. Vital nourishment is being robbed from your body and could set patterns in motion that can take a lifetime to readjust. Start by acknowledging that excessive eating, binging, purging, avoidance of or repulsion for food are not healthy responses. We live in a very food-conscious, abundant society. On the other hand, we are daily bombarded with messages and images of what success should look like.

To train oneself in balanced eating takes time and a change in one's mind-set. Understanding what the deepest "hunger" of one's soul is is necessary, in order to know what the warning signs are.

Over the years, my many conversations with those battling these issues have shown me that it is a problem that manifests itself across gender lines. The overemphasis, in our society, for both males and females to look like ravishing Grecian gods has added pressure to life. I write as one who has been in this prison and now knows what freedom is like.

Epilogue

When I was about nine years old, my sister and I would compare the scars we had on our arms and legs. These were our "battle scars" from climbing through underbrush on the hillside near our house, looking for the right place to build a fort. There were other scars, from the trapeze acts we would do on our bicycles. One of us would pedal, while the other would try a pirouette on the baggage carrier. We had bumps and scrapes from the playground swing and merry-go-round. Most of those scars disappeared over time, but a few could have earned us medal-of-honor status because they were still visible, even after several months.

The scars and wounds on our soul serve as a reminder of where we have been. Not all that has gone before deserves a medal of honor status, but, as the healing presence of God is allowed into these festering places, real healing can come from the inside out.

In Isaiah's portrait of the Suffering Servant, he describes what Jesus did on the cross. He said, *"By his scourging we are healed."* The incredible depth of the wounds that were inflicted upon Jesus has allowed healing to come into the depth of my soul. It is healing for the surface, superficial wounds, but even more so, for those deep gashes that looked irreparable. Jesus has the right ointment to anoint those ragged and torn edges, to make them come back into realignment, health, and wholeness. It may leave a soft, pink scar as a reminder of His incredible healing love, but that's okay.

> *I was wandering in a wilderness, hungry and thirsty;*
> *my soul was fainting within me.*
> *I was dwelling in darkness and in the shadow of death,*

Mirror, Mirror: A Reflected Life

a prisoner in misery and chains because I had rebelled against God's words and counsel.
I was rebellious and abhorred all kinds of food.
Deliverance came when I cried to the L<small>ORD</small> in my trouble and my distress.
He satisfied my thirsty heart and filled my hungry soul with what is good.
He brought me out of darkness and broke the band of death and destruction.
He sent His Word and healed me.
Psalm 107:17-20, My Paraphrase

This reality has filled me with an eternal gratitude toward God. It has released in me a deeper understanding of His loving-kindness and grace. It has confirmed His ability to take the broken pieces of life and restore them to a wholeness that reflects Himself. It has established in me a profound security and resilience from which life flows.

Part II

Poems

Mirror, Mirror: A Reflected Life

DAUGHTER OF ZION

Arise, daughter of Zion, awaken the dawn with your laughter and joy, for the Redeemer has anointed you to go up in procession into the House of the Lord.

His cleansing blood has made you an equal heir with the sons of Adam.

Shake off the shroud of history and tradition, which have captured you and withheld you from the freedom — freedom that has been purchased, not based on gender, but birthed out of the Father's heart.

Arise, daughter of Zion, awaken the dawn with your laughter and joy.

Enter into fellowship and relationship.

Cultivate a teachable spirit, to receive impartation, to impart the immeasurable treasures that are found in the Lord.

Do not vie or compete for favor, for your Redeemer is strong for battle.

Instead, clothe yourself with humility and silence; this is the rabbinical call to any student.

Truly, beloved daughter, you are a gift and not a curse.

Your presence brings edification.

Your understanding and wisdom use for the building up of the Body, discerning what is Truth.

Arise, daughter of Zion, awaken the dawn with your laughter and joy.

Allow the Master's hand to form you.

Allow the coal from the altar to touch your lips, to

Poems

be holy, set apart, empowered to speak out with boldness.
Let His kiss of fellowship enable you to find your place of destiny.
Shake off the chains of opinions formed by thoughts from long ago.
You are genuinely loved in the Beloved.
His redemption has qualified you, as a full inheritor of the Promise.
March on with dignity, casting aside all that would hinder you.
Join the ranks of the many thousands, marching, marching over the land, declaring the Truth.
Arise, daughter of Zion, awaken the dawn with your laughter and joy.

About the Poem

This poem was composed as a response to the story you have just read. I asked the Lord to show me how He saw me as a woman. How does He view us? After writing these words down, I later realized that all of the lines had scripture references.

The poem is like a puzzle, which you will have to work through to get to the deeper treasures. Take time to go back and reread it, using the following references to meditate on. There is so much more in store for you!

¶

You are being given an invitation to be part of a great family. It doesn't matter where you have come from or what your background or past has been, Jesus is offering to make you His daughter.

Mirror, Mirror: A Reflected Life

Zechariah 9:9—*Rejoice greatly, O Daughter of Zion!*

Isaiah 62:11—*Say to the Daughter of Zion, "See, your Savior comes!"*

Zephaniah 3:14-15—*Sing, O Daughter of Zion; shout aloud, O Israel! Be glad and rejoice with all your heart, O Daughter of Jerusalem! The Lord has taken away your punishment, he has turned back your enemy.*

¶

The main emotion in Heaven is gladness. Smiling will not be required; it will be inevitable.

Psalm 16:11—*You have made known to me the path of life; you will fill me with joy in your presence, with eternal pleasures at your right hand.*

Psalm 21:6—*Surely you have granted him blessings and made him glad with the joy of your presence.*

¶

You will awaken the dawn!

Psalm 57:8—*Awake, my soul! Awake, harp and lyre! I will awaken the dawn.*

¶

Go up in procession into the house of the Lord.

Psalm 84:4—*Blessed are those who dwell in your house; they are ever praising you.*

¶

When God created humanity, He chose to portray Himself in two people — a man and a woman. From the very beginning of creation, God's heart radiated dignity to women as they represented a part of Himself that was

Poems

not portrayed in a man. In the same way, a man portrays a facet of God that the woman doesn't. Together they were made in the very image of God.

Genesis 1:27—*So God created man in his own image, in the image of God he created him; male and female he created them.*

Salvation through faith in Jesus Christ is available to all who receive Him.

John 1:12—*Yet to all who received him, to those who believed in his name, he gave the right to become children of God.*

¶

What a joy to know that we have been made clean from the inside out through what Jesus did for us on the cross. All of our sins, both the open and the hidden ones, are forgiven. This means that you don't need to hide anymore. You can come to Jesus and repent and receive a clean heart. To repent means to turn around and to leave the old behind.

Ephesians 1:7—*In him we have redemption through his blood, the forgiveness of sins, in accordance with the riches of God's grace.*

¶

You have received an inheritance.

Ephesians 1:3—*Praise be to the God and Father of our Lord Jesus Christ, who has blessed us in the heavenly realms with every spiritual blessing in Christ.*

Colossians 1:12—*Giving thanks to the Father, who has qualified you to share in the inheritance of the saints in the kingdom of light.*

Mirror, Mirror: A Reflected Life

Acts 20:32—*Now I commit you to God and to the word of his grace, which can build you up and give you an inheritance among all those who are sanctified.*

An inheritance implies that you:

* Belong
* Have a name
* Have a future
* Have a hope
* Have provision
* Have significance
* Are part of a bigger family

¶

We are all affected and formed by the opinions of those who surround us. Ideas we have learned do not always bring freedom to our spirits. True freedom means a deep understanding of what it means to be transformed from the inside out.

Colossians 2:8—*See to it that no one takes you captive through hollow and deceptive philosophy, which depends on human tradition and the basic principles of this world rather than on Christ.*

Galatians 5:1—*It is for freedom that Christ has set us free. Stand firm, then, and do not let yourselves be burdened again by a yoke of slavery.*

The Gospel is very accessible and simple.

* God so loved the whole world that He gave His Son.

John 3:16—*For God so loved the world that he gave his one and only Son, that whoever believes in him shall not perish but have eternal life.*

* All have sinned and come short of God's standard.

Poems

Romans 3:23—*For all have sinned and fall short of the glory of God.*

* If we confess with our mouth that Jesus is Lord and believe in our heart that God raised Him from the dead, we shall be saved.

Romans 10:9-10—*If you confess with your mouth, "Jesus is Lord," and believe in your heart that God raised him from the dead, you will be saved. For it is with your heart that you believe and are justified, and it is with your mouth that you confess and are saved.*

¶

We have received this new life, not just to keep it to ourselves, but also to share it with others around us. One of the first steps is to be a learner, a student of God's Word. Take time to read and meditate on the Bible. Meditation is like the process of digesting your food. If your body doesn't digest its food well, then it will not get the nutrients that are needed. When you meditate on God's Word, you think about what you have read and allow the Holy Spirit to help you process and absorb it.

Psalm 1:2—*But his delight is in the law of the LORD, and on his law he meditates day and night.*

¶

Have a teachable spirit.

James 4:10—*Humble yourselves in the presence of the Lord, and He will exalt you* (NASB).

2 Timothy 2:15—*Do your best to present yourself to God as one approved, a workman who does not need to be ashamed and who correctly handles the word of truth.*

Isaiah 50:4—*The Sovereign Lord has given me an instructed tongue, to know the word that sustains the weary.*

Mirror, Mirror: A Reflected Life

He wakens my ear to listen like one being taught.

Psalm 119:9-11—*How can a young man keep his way pure? By living according to your word. I seek you with all my heart; do not let me stray from your commands. I have hidden your word in my heart that I might not sin against you.*

¶

There is no competition in the Kingdom of God. Jesus has a unique place for each of us. We are all gifted differently, and with these gifts we can glorify God.

1 Peter 2:9—*But you are a chosen people, a royal priesthood, a holy nation, a people belonging to God, that you may declare the praises of him who called you out of darkness into his wonderful light.*

Ephesians 2:10—*For we are God's workmanship, created in Christ Jesus to do good works, which God prepared in advance for us to do.*

¶

Do not harbor jealousy and envy toward one another in your heart.

James 3:13-16—*Who is wise and understanding among you? Let him show it by his good life, by deeds done in the humility that comes from wisdom. But if you harbor bitter envy and selfish ambition in your hearts, do not boast about it or deny the truth. Such "wisdom" does not come down from heaven but is earthly, unspiritual, of the devil. For where you have envy and selfish ambition, there you find disorder and every evil practice.*

¶

The Lord is on your side, fighting for you, not against you. He wants to comfort you in His love.

Poems

Zephaniah 3:17—*The LORD your God is with you, he is mighty to save. He will take great delight in you, he will quiet you with his love, he will rejoice over you with singing.*

¶

There is a time and place to talk to God, but also to listen to what He wants to say. Take the time to be taught by the Lord.

Psalm 25:4—*Show me your ways, O LORD, teach me your paths.*

Psalm 27:11—*Teach me your way, O LORD; lead me in a straight path.*

Psalm 143:10—*Teach me to do your will, for you are my God; may your good Spirit lead me on level ground.*

¶

You are so lovely in the eyes of the Lord. He looks at you with dignity, worth, love and true affection.

Song of Songs 1:15—*How beautiful you are, my darling!*

Psalm 149:4—*For the LORD takes delight in his people; he crowns the humble with salvation.*

Psalm 139:14—*I praise you because I am fearfully and wonderfully made; your works are wonderful, I know that full well.*

¶

You are loved. A great price has been paid for you. What an honor and privilege to be the daughter of the highest God! His love is an act of grace.

Ephesians 2:8-9—*For it is by grace you have been saved, through faith — and this not from yourselves, it is the gift of God — not by works so that no one can boast.*

Mirror, Mirror: A Reflected Life

Use what you have received to build up others.

Ephesians 4:12—*To prepare God's people for works of service, so that the body of Christ may be built up.*

Proverbs 14:1—*The wise woman builds her house, but with her own hands the foolish tears hers down.*

¶

We are like clay in the Potter's hands. He is forming and making us into a choice vessel for His use.

Jeremiah 18:6—*"O house of "Israel, can I not do with you as this potter does?" declares the Lord. "Like clay in the hand of the potter, so are you in my hand, O house of Israel."*

¶

Allow the Holy Spirit to cleanse and touch your lips. How we speak brings either death or life to those who listen. May our words be channels of encouragement.

Proverbs 18:21—*The tongue has the power of life and death.*

Proverbs 13:3—*The one who guards his mouth preserves his life.* (NASB)

Psalm 34:12-13—*Whoever of you loves life and desires to see many good days, keep your tongue from evil and your lips from speaking lies.*

¶

The Lord gives us His kiss of friendship. What an honor to have the seal of love upon us! It is His love which cannot be broken that enables us to go on.

Song of Songs 1:2—*Let him kiss me with the kisses of his mouth — for your love is more delightful than wine.*

Poems

Romans 8:38-39—*For I am convinced that neither death nor life, neither angels nor demons, neither the present nor the future, nor any powers, neither height nor depth, nor anything else in all creation, will be able to separate us from the love of God that is in Christ Jesus our Lord.*

¶

You are carrying this seed of promise. The Holy Spirit will enable you to go where He leads.

Matthew 28:18-20—*All authority has been given to me in heaven and on earth. Go therefore and make disciples of all nations, baptizing them in the name of the Father and of the Son and of the Holy Spirit, teaching them to observe all that I have commanded you; and lo, I am with you always, even to the end of the age.* (NASB)

Revelation 7:17—*For the Lamb at the center of the throne will be their shepherd; he will lead them to springs of living water. And God will wipe away every tear from their eyes.*

Together with the prophetess Deborah, we can speak to our heart to arise and march on with strength.

Judges 5:21—*March on my soul; be strong.*

There is a crowd of fellow travellers who are proclaiming the wonderful news of deliverance. The invitation is to come and join them.

Psalm 68:11—*The Lord announced the word, and great was the company of those who proclaimed it.*

Because the Lord is our strength, we do not have to fear!

Exodus 15:2—*The LORD is my strength and my song; he has become my salvation.*

Mirror, Mirror: A Reflected Life

IMAGE BEARER

Image bearer of the Most High, your radiance shines like the Morning Star.

Your countenance resembles your Maker, yet toil and sweat has become your portion, despite your place as heir to the King.

Your muscles and strength are compared on the battlefield of life, as you wrestle, warring for a place on the top of the heap.

Value is placed on the acquisition of possessions, immaterial to the worthiness of the conquest.

Mammon, Mannine[1] and Monopoly have become your idols of choice.

Image bearer of the Most High, you have been created for so much more.

The exuberance and adventure of your heart sings for a place where affirmation is given, based on who you are, not what you do.

Your masculinity is a worthy gift, to enable you to reconnect with your Maker.

His desire is not to tame you, or emasculate you, but to truly love you.

And for you to know His fatherly embrace.

Together with the daughters of Zion, you have been created as an equal heir to the Promise, for your shame to be covered with His forgiveness, wholeness and wellness to your soul.

Image bearer of the Most High, avoid the teachings

---

1   *Mannine* appears in various Dutch translations of the Bible, meaning Eve. The author's intent here was to indicate the evils of money, sex and power.

Poems

and traditions that would encourage you to divide and plunder, calling upon your unredeemed instincts to pacify your ego.

The One who you are called to emulate is both the Lion and the Lamb.

These do not war against each other, but bring to fulfillment the wildness that is in your heart.

Image bearer of the Most High, find your place of rest in the intimacy of His embrace, for He knows you by your true name.

Part III

Meditations

Meditations on the Word

Transformation starts to take place when our thinking is changed. Through the narration of my story, this process was underlined. There are so many little lies or wrong thought patterns, which, when held up against the truth of God's Word, are exposed for what they really are.

These are the wrong building stones in our foundation, which need to be exchanged for truth. The following meditations address some key areas of our thinking:

* How do I view God? Is He really trustworthy?
* What source do I draw my significance from?
* What is my life focus?
* What are the walls that keep my heart compartmentalized?
* Is it possible to develop a life of prayer?
* Is it possible to receive divine guidance in my life?
* If wisdom means learning the skill in living, how do I start to acquire this?

A meditation is an invitation to take the time to ponder and think about what is being said. The renewal of the mind starts to happen when the truth, from God's Word, is applied in life.

Meditations

THE ROOTED LIFE (BASED ON PSALM 1)

How blessed is the man who does not walk in the counsel of the wicked,
Nor stand in the path of sinners,
Nor sit in the seat of scoffers!
But his delight is in the law of the LORD,
And in His law he meditates day and night.
He will be like a tree firmly planted by streams of water,
Which yields its fruit in season
And its leaf does not wither;
And, in whatever he does, he prospers.

The wicked are not,
But they are like chaff which the wind drives away. Therefore the wicked will not stand in the judgment,
Nor sinners in the assembly of the righteous.
For the Lord knows the way of the righteous,
But the way of the wicked will perish. (NASB)

The Bible is full of images, metaphors and similes to help us grasp some of its deeper truths. Here we read of a person whose life was so rooted that it was characterized by continual fruitfulness. Not only that, but this life did not succumb to dryness, and its leaves never withered. This short psalm gives us some valuable clues as to how to develop an intimate relationship with God.

Strong roots, like these, do not grow in a day, as it takes time and investment. But where do we start? What can we learn from this image?

Mirror, Mirror: A Reflected Life

A seed will germinate and take root when it is planted in a conducive environment. In order for the seed of the Gospel to find its lodging place in our hearts, there are some foundational questions we need to ask ourselves and then find the answers so that growth can take place.

Can I really trust God? What is He like? I will only entrust my life to someone I trust because I find them to be trustworthy. Learning to trust God will mean the difference between living a life filled with doubt and unbelief or hope.

What motivates God to do what He does anyway? The answer that I find to this question will either make me feel loved or rejected.

Is God really strong enough to take my anxieties, worries and cares from me? The answer here will lead to a life that is characterized by either fear or faith.

How I view God's character, motivation and ability will affect how I answer these questions. It will affect how I live my life, exercise my worship and the prayers that I pray, and how I determine the direction my life should take.

From the earliest accounts of mankind's fall into sin, as recorded in Genesis, these three questions were used by Satan to call into question the reliability of God, His nature and character, His word and His actions.

God reveals Himself in irrefutable words, when He says of Himself that He is gracious, compassionate, slow to anger, abounding in loving-kindness, that he is faithful, just and true (see Exodus 34:6-7). My faulty understanding of God may need to be readjusted to the plumb line of His revealed Word. This revelation

Meditations

of God's character enables me to trust Him and have hope, as hope is based on the reliability of God's character.

The eternal paradigm of God's motivation is captured in John 3:16, where we read: *"For God so loved the world that he gave his one and only Son ..."* God's love motivated Him to give His best. This love was deep enough to embrace the agony and suffering of a rebellious world and follow through with the plan of redemption (God gave His Son, Jesus, to die on the cross, so that the chasm of separation between Him and me could be bridged). If my life is filled with moments of feeling unloved or rejected, this picture is enough to call my heart back to reality to embrace the truth that I am loved.

If I doubt God's ability to do what He says He is able to do, I will always need a plan B ready to escape to. I will also live a life characterized more by fear than faith. Psalm 55:22 calls us to: *"Cast your burden upon the* Lord *and He will sustain you"* (NASB). I don't need to deny the anxious thoughts of fear, but, rather, acknowledge them and entrust them into the strong arms of God.

When I know that the God of the Bible is true to His word, reliable, trustworthy, loving and able, then His words can take root in my heart, causing a sturdy, durable, flourishing tree to grow. This tree draws deeply from the stream of living water that Jesus refers to in John 7. The outpouring of God's Spirit within our innermost being is this vibrant stream, and we can draw from it.

The food and nutrients for this resilient spiritual life are found in the meditation on God's Word (law). This

Mirror, Mirror: A Reflected Life

process of meditation is taking the Word, pondering on it, applying it, internalizing it, and not compromising on it. This will lead to growth, strength and fruitfulness.

We have been given an invitation to come to the Source, to put down roots, to become resilient people who can stand despite or in the face of whatever life circumstances come our way.

To Ponder:
* Have I allowed the *"seed of the Gospel,"* according to Jesus' reference to the Word, to take root in my heart?
* A seed needs to *"die"* to itself in order to become what it was intended to be. Reflect on these verses:

John 12:24-26—*Truly, truly, I say to you, unless a grain of wheat falls into the earth and dies, it remains alone; but if it dies, it bears much fruit. He who loves his life loses it, and he who hates his life in this world will keep it to life eternal. If anyone serves Me, he must follow Me; and where I am, there My servant will be also; if anyone serves Me, the Father will honor him.* (NASB)

Galatians 2:20—*I have been crucified with Christ and I no longer live, but Christ lives in me. The life I live in the body, I live by faith in the Son of God, who loved me and gave himself for me.*

* Take time to reflect on God's character, motivation and ability.

To Reflect On:

Jeremiah 17:7-8—*Blessed is the man who trusts in the* L<small>ORD</small>, *whose confidence is in him. He will be like a*

Meditations

tree planted by the water that sends out its roots by the stream. It does not fear when heat comes; its leaves are always green. It has no worries in a year of drought and never fails to bear fruit.

Colossians 2:6-7—*So then, just as you received Christ Jesus as Lord, continue to live in him, rooted and built up in him, strengthened in the faith as you were taught, and overflowing with thankfulness.*

1 John 4:16-19—*God is love. Whoever lives in love lives in God, and God in him. In this way, love is made complete among us so that we will have confidence on the day of judgment, because in this world we are like him. There is no fear in love. But perfect love drives out fear, because fear has to do with punishment. The one who fears is not made perfect in love. We love because he first loved us.*

1 Corinthians 10:13—*No temptation has seized you except what is common to man. And God is faithful; he will not let you be tempted beyond what you can bear. But when you are tempted, he will also provide a way out so that you can stand up under it.*

Jude 24—*To him who is able to keep you from falling and to present you before his glorious presence without fault and with great joy.*

To Pray:

Lord, thank You for being so reliable and trustworthy. You are so true to Your word and invite me to rest in this knowledge. The *"seed of the Gospel"* that I have received has the potential to turn my life upside down. I can place the weight of my life into Your hands and embrace all that You want to accomplish in me.

Mirror, Mirror: A Reflected Life

The Spirit-Empowered Life (based on Psalm 84)

How lovely are your dwelling places,
O Lord of hosts!
My soul longed and even yearned for the courts of the Lord;
My heart and my flesh sing for joy to the living God [nearness releases intimacy].
The bird also has found a house,
And the swallow a nest for herself, where she may lay her young,
Even Your altars, O Lord of hosts,
My King and my God.
How blessed are those who dwell in Your house!
They are ever praising You [nearness releases worship].

How blessed is the man whose strength is in You,
In whose heart are the highways to Zion!
Passing through the valley of Baca [weeping] *they make it a spring* [nearness releases transformation]*;*
The early rain also covers it with blessings.
They go from strength to strength [nearness releases strength]*,*
Every one of them appears before God in Zion.

O Lord God of hosts, hear my prayer;
Give ear, O God of Jacob! Selah.
Behold our shield, O God,
And look upon the face of Your anointed.
For a day in Your courts is better than a thousand outside.

Meditations

I would rather stand at the threshold of the house of my God
Than dwell in the tents of wickedness.
*For the L*ORD *God is a sun and shield;*
*The L*ORD *gives grace and glory* [nearness releases the gifts]*;*
No good thing does He withhold from those who walk uprightly.
*O L*ORD *of hosts,*
How blessed is the man who trusts in You! (NASB)

Nearness Is Based on Trust!

Many of us try to be faithful disciples on our own without the power of the Holy Spirit. The vital, electrifying work of the Holy Spirit is missing. The truth is that God wants to be active in all of our lives, to endue us with the supernatural. Jesus made it clear that the Holy Spirit would be sent to live within us. Our task is to find ways to be open to the energizing work of the living God. No one can really live the Christian life without the Holy Spirit.

In this psalm we find some keys which will help us better understand how to embark on this journey of the Spirit-empowered life. They will enable us to live life as God intended it to be lived.

In looking at Psalm 84, we observe what happens when we truly come home to the Father.

Nearness Releases Intimacy

This journey can only begin as we come home to the Father and dwell in His presence. This is an invitation for the Lord to come into every area of our lives. There

Mirror, Mirror: A Reflected Life

is nothing hidden from Him. He knows our every secret, desire, failure and victory. His job description is to guide us into all truth; He brings people to the truth of God.

The Spirit is an advocate who comes alongside to plead our case. His origin is that He comes from the Father in the name of Jesus, and His character is to teach us the truth and give us wise counsel.

The Holy Spirit enables us to learn how to pray, discern our spiritual gifts, and bear *"the fruit of the Spirit."* Aside from the convicting work of the Holy Spirit, a person would never see himself or herself as a sinner. Only the Holy Spirit can reveal that a righteous status before God does not depend on good works, but on Christ's death on the cross.

To live out Christ's teachings requires the enabling presence of His Spirit. The nature of the Holy Spirit is to be with us forever, abiding with us, abiding in us, and testifying about Jesus. The Holy Spirit witnesses to our spirit that the Good News (that Jesus was born, lived, died, and rose again from the dead) is true, and He prompts us to accept it.

Nearness Releases Worship

What is worship? It is the believer's response to God's revelation of Himself. It includes yielding to God, as Lord and Master, adorning God, admiring Him, appreciating Him, letting Him know how grateful we are for His mighty works and the blessings He bestows. Worship is the appropriate response to who God is, what He gives, what He does, and what He promises.

Praise is not dependent upon circumstances, but an opportunity to refocus the heart on God's goodness and

Meditations

greatness. He will forever be worthy of our adoration. Praising God in the midst of trials is not denying our feelings, but a choice to lift our attention to Him who holds all things in His hands. God is looking for those who will worship Him in spirit and in truth. Learning how to worship here on earth is a "dress rehearsal for heaven." Praise brings us into His presence and brings down His glory.

The importance of praise is that it strengthens and gives expression to our faith. Trust is the basic response God is looking for. Faith moves God to reveal Himself more clearly to us. We were made to bring Him pleasure and praise pleases Him.

Nearness Brings Transformation

What does a Spirit-filled walk mean? It implies walking in liberty. It means walking, not sitting; it is not a passive life, sitting back and waiting for God to do it all. Walking in the Spirit implies walking, not running. Walking in the Spirit implies walking by being led. A Spirit-filled walk will be evidenced by the fruit it bears. It is not dependent upon the circumstances. In fact it enables the one who is passing through incredibly hard circumstances to turn their desert into a place of springs.

Trials rip away the flimsy fabric of our self-sufficiency. This makes room for God's Spirit to weave into our life a true and solid confidence.

Philippians 4:13—*I can do everything through him who gives me strength.*

Fire separates scum from both silver and gold. When we cooperate with the Holy Spirit, He removes the scum in our character, transforming us more into God's likeness.

Nearness Releases Strength

The Holy Spirit is all that you need for life and godliness. He inspires praise, comfort, encouragement, and inexpressible joy, and He gives strength in the innermost being, power to both love and serve. You don't have to beg to be filled, for He is eager to do it for you. You don't earn His fullness, proving you are worthy, because all you need to do is allow the Spirit to fill you, by consenting to live under His gracious influence and control.

Through praise you focus your attention back on God. You acknowledge Him as your Source of overcoming power. You can see your problems from a new perspective. It is in this moment that His strength arises within us. When we wait on the Lord, our strength is renewed.

Isaiah 40:30-31—*Even youths grow tired and weary, and young men stumble and fall; but those who hope in the LORD will renew their strength. They will soar on wings like eagles; they will run and not grow weary, they will walk and not be faint.*

Nearness Releases the Gifts

The Lord has gifts that He wants to bestow on each one of us. These blessings cannot be earned, but are freely given by God to His children. A gift is a sign of relationship, not a reward for good behavior. Gifts are not to guide our lives but to help unfold God to us. They help us in our response to Him and create in us a healthy fear of the Lord.

Meditations

God is the One who enrolls us in the School of the Spirit. He has things to teach us before He can trust us more fully in this area.

God delights in doing miracles and using His children in this way. Gifts are for the building up of the Body of Christ. God wants the gifts to be active in the Christian's life, to increase our own joy and also to make it clear to the world that Jesus is alive and real. The Holy Spirit divides the gifts to every believer as He wills, and the Holy Spirit wills that we live an abundant life in Christ.

Nearness Is Based on Trust, Which Empowers Us To Live Life as God Intended

We do not live our lives under our own steam. We were never created to do this. We were created to live life in cooperation with another reality, life in and through the Spirit of God. We grow in this area by yielding to the work of the Spirit, by surrendering ourselves to God. Open the door of your spirit so that He can come in and begin to change the way you think and live. This may lead to a time of confession. Nurture the fruit of the Spirit.

Galatians 5:22-23—*But the fruit of the Spirit is love, joy, peace, patience, kindness, goodness, faithfulness, gentleness and self-control. Against such things there is no law.*

Fruit grows without making a sound. Therefore we can miss so much of what it could be in our lives, if we do not pay attention to cultivate it. Set time aside and meditate on the fruit of the Spirit. Ask God to show you which virtue needs to be more evident in your life. Ask the Holy Spirit to begin to work in your mind and heart, knowing that change comes by sustained communion with God.

Mirror, Mirror: A Reflected Life

To Ponder:
* Describe what it means for you to "dwell" or be "at home" in God's presence.
* Are there areas where you want Him to change the "valley of weeping" into a "well-spring"?
* Take time to tell the Lord how grateful you are for His transforming power in your life.

To Pray:

Father, thank You for welcoming me "home," to be with You, live with You and, from this place of security, to step out into the world around me. Thank You for the deep worship that is released within my life as I spend time with You. Thank You for Your transforming power to change the deep "valleys" of trouble in my life into a place of blessing and joy. I trust You with my life.

Meditations

THE FOCUSED LIFE (BASED ON PSALM 27:8)

My heart says of you, "Seek his face!"
Your face, LORD, I will seek.

When we are in love with someone, we really want to study his or her face. We want to get to know the subtleties that show us what the other is thinking. The following scriptures invite us to embark on this journey of getting to know the contours of the face of our heavenly Father.

Psalm 11:7—*For the LORD is righteous, he loves justice; upright men will see his face.*

Psalm 17:15—*And I, in righteousness I will see your face; when I awake, I shall be satisfied with seeing your likeness.*

Psalm 30:7—*When you hide your face, I was dismayed.*

What do we see when we look into someone's face? We are generally attracted to their eyes. What we see in a person's eyes either encourages us to pursue further communication or not. God is seeking intimacy with us: *"into me see."* But what do I see when I gaze into His eyes?

Psalm 34:15—*The eyes of the LORD are on the righteous.*

Psalm 33:13—*From heaven the LORD looks down and sees all mankind.*

Psalm 33:18—*But the eyes of the LORD are on those who fear him, on those whose hope is in his unfailing love.*

Psalm 17:8—*Keep me as the apple of your eye.*

2 Chronicles 16:9—*For the eyes of the LORD range*

Mirror, Mirror: A Reflected Life

throughout the earth to strengthen those whose hearts are fully committed to him.

Psalm 32:8—*I will instruct you and teach you in the way that you should go; I will counsel you and watch over you.*

God is like a coach who knows where each player is and can help us stay on track when we have our focus on Him. The Lord desires that we be aware of the fact that He sees us. He looks at us with eyes of care, compassion, comfort, counsel, and correction. Images and echoes of memories of the stern, unloving eyes of those who have hurt us in the past need to be replaced by the image of the Father who is seeking for us.

In the story of the prodigal son (see Luke 15:11-31), it was the Father who remained on the lookout to see if his son would return. The father did not know of the son's intention to find his way home again, but the father had hoped, anticipated, yearned to have the reunion take place. He positioned himself to await the moment that he would see his son on the horizon. In that same way, our Father is eagerly waiting to make eye contact with us.

When we gaze into the Father's eyes, what do we hear from His mouth? What we hear will determine how we speak and what we believe about who we are.

Psalm 32:7 says: *"You ... surround me with songs of deliverance."* Have we heard the Lord singing over us? Have our ears caught this melody of freedom? Can we pick up the tune and sing these songs over ourselves and others?

The Lord is singing over us (see Zephaniah 3:17). May our ears be tuned and open to hear His songs. As Song of Solomon 1:2 says: *"May he kiss me with the kisses of his mouth."* Have we felt His kiss of affirmation on our foreheads?

Meditations

Luke 3:22—*You are my Son, whom I love; with you I am well pleased.*

These were the first words that Jesus heard the Father speak over Him at His baptism, and the Lord is speaking and singing these same words over His earthly children as well.

Psalm 5:1-3—*Give ear to my words, O LORD, consider my sighing. Listen to my cry for help, my King and my God, for to you I pray. In the morning, O Lord, you hear my voice; morning by morning I lay my requests before you and wait in expectation.*

God's ears are not deaf to our cry. He hears our whimpering sobs and our joyous shouts alike. He shares in our laughter and our pleas.

To Ponder:
- Have you given the Father the echoes of your past?
- Have you heard the Father's song of deliverance sung over your life?
- Have you learned how to pick up His "tune" and sing it out over the lives of others around you?

To Pray:

Lord, thank You for Your song of life and jubilee that You are singing over me. Sometimes it is like an angelic choir, and other times it is more a whispered lullaby. Teach my heart to sing these new tunes to a world in desperate need to hear the song of the Father.

Mirror, Mirror: A Reflected Life

THE TRANSFORMED LIFE (BASED ON PSALM 86:11)

Teach me your way, O LORD, and I will walk in your truth;
give me an undivided heart, that I may fear your name.

Like the many doors that are in a house, there are many compartments in my heart. There are areas which are open to both myself and others, and that is where I live my everyday life. These areas are easily accessible. On a regular basis, I need grace to fill this space in my heart.

But these do not form the whole picture; I have another place where I keep my secrets. These are the things that have trapped me in guilt and shame, which I find hard to deal with and have often buried very deeply. I take special effort and use much emotional energy to make sure that these secrets are kept in the dungeon of my heart, hoping that no one will look at or guess at what has gone on in the past. This area needs to receive the mercy and forgiveness of the Lord.

I also have a compartment that is hidden to me but very obvious to those who live around me. I could call this my "blind spot," and this needs to be exposed by others, in order for patterns to change. What is needed is the light and love of the Father to help me deal with what is found here.

There is also a domain inside of me that I and others are clueless to. This is the area where vows, judgments, and decisions have been made in the past and then forgotten. They act like the fine print on a contract, binding me to certain rules on how to live, even long after I have forgotten about them. This is the area where the Holy Spirit needs to bring deep revelation and healing.

This psalm is a prayer, an invitation, to the Lord to tear down the walls that keep various parts of me hidden from sight. As

Meditations

the segments of my heart receive the restoring touch of the Father, He releases to me the ability to walk in the fear of the Lord. This is nothing more than having a healthy and loving reverence for the Lord, being submitted to His Lordship, and being obedient to His Word.

This prayer was echoed in King David's psalm of confession when he wrote:

> *Create in me a pure heart, oh God, and renew a steadfast spirit within me.* Psalm 51:10

To Ponder:
* Take time to ask the Lord to reveal the "fragmentation" in your heart. Because the Lord is trustworthy, gracious, kind and loving, He is able to heal, restore and renew you from the inside out.
* Take time to look up the amazing promises that are associated with a lifestyle of "walking in the fear of the Lord."
* Take time to read through Psalm 51 as a prayer.

To Pray:

Lord, I echo King David's prayer that You would create in me a clean heart and that You would renew a steadfast spirit within me. Search me, O Lord, and see if there be any hurtful way in me. You desire truth in the innermost being, and I welcome You in my heart of hearts. Unveil my heart to receive Your embrace. I sometimes choose the shadows of self, forgetting that even these areas devoid of light do not hinder You. Your light reveals those areas of compromise, those places where Your glory does not enter. May my heart repeat the cry: "Come, Lord Jesus, Come!"

Mirror, Mirror: A Reflected Life

THE ANCHORED LIFE (BASED ON PSALM 139:1-18)

O LORD, You have searched me and you know me.
You know when I sit down and when I rise; you perceive my thoughts from afar.
You discern my going out and my lying down; you are familiar with all my ways.
Before a word is on my tongue, you know it completely, O LORD.

You hem me in — behind and before, you have laid your hand upon me.
Such knowledge is too wonderful for me, too lofty for me to attain.

Where can I go from your Spirit? Where can I flee from your presence?
If I go up to the heavens, you are there; if I make my bed in the depths, you are there.
If I rise on the wings of the dawn, if I settle on the far side of the sea, even there your hand will guide me, and your right hand will hold me fast.

If I say, "Surely the darkness will hide me, and the light become dark around me,"
even the darkness will not be dark to you, the night will shine like the day, for darkness is as light to you.

For you created my inmost being; you knit me together in my mother's womb.
I praise you because I am fearfully and wonderfully

Meditations

made; your works are wonderful, I know that full well.
My frame was not hidden from you, when I was made in the secret place.
When I was woven together in the depths of the earth, your eyes saw my unformed body.
All the days ordained for me were written in your book before one of them came to be.

How precious to me are your thoughts, O God! How vast is the sum of them!
Were I to count them, they would outnumber the grains of sand.
When I awake, I am still with you.

To know and be known are part of the foundational longings of the human heart. To be known and still be loved is one of the biggest discoveries of life.

This psalm describes the all-encompassing presence of God. He is the One who says that He is there for us. He is our Creator, and our gender is planted deeply within His heart and gives us an anchor for our identity. Our view of Him may have to be adjusted and expanded. Instead of fearing Him looking over our shoulders, we need to see Him as the One who can provide total care and give provision.

His thoughts toward us are of affirmation. Our existence, our life brings pleasure to Him, no matter the circumstances surrounding our conception, birth, or upbringing. The anchor is that I am wanted, desired, known and marveled at.

The sooner I discover in life that I cannot hide from God, the quicker the vacillating torrents of my life will be stabilized. The Lord is even with me when I embark on the journey of dealing with painful issues that have entrapped me. Abuse, abandonment, rejection, addiction, depression or despair do not intimidate Him. The judgment, criticism, or insecurity in my heart, when projected onto others, not only hurts them, but I also wound and injure myself in the process. Secrecy, guilt, and shame are exposed in the light of the fact that I cannot hide from God's searching gaze. He is committed to not leave me the way He finds me.

What a freedom to know that the Lord cares enough about the small details of my life to identify them! He understands why I've done what I've done. He is intimately acquainted with this process and wants to give clarity and revelation to me about it.

Will I allow Him to hug me with His arms of healing, restoration and blessing? Will I allow Him to come close enough to place His hand in affirmation upon my head? He wants to place them there, to bless and anoint and to impart to me the security of being known and loved.

God's invitation to me is to allow Him to search me, to know me, to allow Him to calm my anxious thoughts. Life does not need to be a repetitive treadmill. God is asking us to allow Him to change this pattern in us.

What are the thoughts that God has toward us?
 * He desires that we be free from fear and shame.
 * He wants to restore us into relationship.
 * He wants to give us a future and a hope.
 * His thoughts are for welfare and not for calamity.
 * He longs for us to know that we are loved.
 * He longs for us to know that our sin separates us, but that there is the gift of redemption and

Meditations

restoration that is offered and received through confession and repentance.
* Eye has not seen nor ear heard all that He has prepared for those who love Him.
* He thought of us before the foundation of the world.

To Ponder:
* How does it make you feel that there is no place you can go where the Lord is not present?
* Take time to reflect on the meaning of the text that says that the Lord knew us even before we were born and that He delighted in us even before we had seen the light of day.
* Review the scriptures about the thoughts that God has toward us.

To Pray:
Lord, thank You for loving me so much that You know all about me, yet still love me. Thank You for being with me from the moment of conception until now. I am not alone, and that knowledge fills me with joy and gladness. Thank You for thinking thoughts of welfare and not of calamity over my life.

Mirror, Mirror: A Reflected Life

THE GUIDED LIFE (BASED ON PSALM 25:3-5, 9 AND 12-15)

No one whose hope is in you will ever be put to shame, but they will be put to shame who are treacherous without excuse. Show me your ways, O Lord, teach me your paths; guide me in your truth and teach me, for you are God my Savior, and my hope is in you all day long.
He guides the humble in what is right and teaches them his way.
Who, then, is the man that fears the Lord? He will instruct him in the way chosen for him. He will spend his days in prosperity, and his descendants will inherit the land. The Lord confides in those who fear him; he makes his covenant known to them. My eyes are ever on the Lord, for only he will release my feet from the snare.

The Lord has promised that we will find the path to life when we seek Him. He has promised us that we will not be ashamed when we put our confidence in Him. The request that we read in this psalm is echoed throughout the Bible, the desire is to be taught, instructed and given understanding as to how to take the next steps in life. One of the primary ways to grow in this is to develop a lifestyle of prayer.

The disciples of Jesus worded this in a very powerful way when they asked Him to teach them how to pray (see Luke 11:1). Prayer is communication and communion with God. It involves not only talking, but also listening to what He has to say. The prayer that Jesus

Meditations

taught His disciples is like a text-message. It is short and concise, but has all of the ingredients that are needed to grow in this area of hearing what the Lord has to say.

Prayer is the doorway into relationship with God. When we come to Him, we need to know that He is not arbitrary but trustworthy. He has taken the initiative to come to us. He longs for fellowship. God desires relationship, to reveal to us His character, His purposes, and His ways. It is about growing in relationship and not about reciting a formula.

We will look at this prayer line by line.

> *Our Father in heaven,*
> *hallowed be your name,*
> *your kingdom come,*
> *your will be done on earth as it is in heaven.*
> *Give us today our daily bread.*
> *Forgive us our debts, as we also have forgiven our debtors.*
> *And lead us not into temptation, but deliver us from the evil one.*

The NASB adds:
For Yours is the kingdom and the power and the glory forever. Amen. Matthew 6:9-13

Our Father

By starting with *"our Father,"* Jesus addresses a primal need in each human being. Biologically, we have all been fathered, but emotionally and physically this may have been, for us, the greatest source of pain, lack, and abuse and the cause of some of our deepest wounds.

Mirror, Mirror: A Reflected Life

In God, we meet the perfect Father, who has the highest interest in us and views us with esteem and value. He relates to us with perfect love, is never absent, preoccupied or disinterested. His thoughts over us are for welfare and not for calamity, to give us hope and a future. In Him the broken images of the past can be restored. He is above all else and does not derive His name from any other.

A father provides a name, legitimacy, status, a sense of belonging, and an inheritance. Although our present situation may lack all of these things, the invitation, at the start of this prayer, is to come and enter into a relationship with the Father.

In the ensuing chapters of the Gospels, Jesus elaborates further as to how to enter into this relationship. He said, in John 14:6, *"I am the way, and the truth, and the life; no one comes to the Father but through Me"* (NASB). John 1:12 says: *"As many as received him, to them he gave the right to become children of God, even to those who believe in His name"* (NASB). The first step is to enter into this relationship with our heavenly Father, to receive the initial healing of restoration, redemption, focus, and hope.

Who Art in Heaven

God is not a figment of our imagination, but He occupies real time, space, and history. This does not denote distance, but a clarification that He has no equal. God is not a created being. In Him is all that there is and all that there ever will be. He is outside of the created order, although, through Jesus, He became flesh and dwelt among us, therefore, His creative power and ability is not limited to the resources we see around us.

Meditations

We come to God in prayer because He is the Source above every other source. Because of the fact that He is who He is, miracles can happen. His perspective is so much greater than ours, and He always has the bigger picture in mind. I cannot bog Him down with my questions, worries, and concerns. When I come to Him in prayer, He can lift me up, to see what I could not see before.

Hallowed Be Your Name

Hallowed means "holy, set apart, pure, undefiled." In the Jewish culture, names have great significance. A name describes someone, says something about who they are or what they represent. I personally have various names: my given name is Carolyn, my childhood name (that stuck for many years) was Kari, my husband calls me Lieverd (Sweetheart), my children call me Mom, my grandchildren call me Nana. I am one and the same person, but each name reveals more of who I am and who I relate to.

In the initial pages of the Bible, God introduces Himself, as a trinity (three in one). As the chapters go on, He reveals more of His character by revealing His various names. When you study the Bible, you will discover many more names that describe other facets of God's nature and character.

Proverbs 18:10—*The name of the Lord is a strong tower; the righteous run to it and are safe.*

His name is so secure and offers safety. Knowing this can get our focus off of ourselves and onto the One who is mighty to save.

Psalm 9:10 (NASB) says: *"Those who know Your name will put their trust in You."*

Mirror, Mirror: A Reflected Life

Knowing His name is vital in order for our trust in Him to grow. Here are a few of the names that are used to describe who the Lord is and why His name is a strong tower:

* Jehovah-Jirah (Provider) — Genesis 22
* Jehovah-Rapha (Healer) — Exodus 15:26
* Jehovah-Shalom (Peace) — Judges 6:24
* Jehovah-Nissi (Banner) — Exodus 17:15
* Jehovah-Ra'ah (Shepherd) — Psalm 23:1;
* Jehovah-Tsidkenu (Righteousness) — Jeremiah 33:16
* Jehovah-Shammah (Ever-Abiding Presence) — Ezekiel 48:35
* Jehovah-M'Kaddesh (Sanctification, to be made holy) — Leviticus 20:8

In *Jesus* we are introduced to the name above all names, as in the name of Jesus there is power to save (see Philippians 2:9-11). Take time to meditate on the names of God. Ask the Holy Spirit to show you what His names mean to you in your life situations.

Your Kingdom Come, Your Will Be Done

Life is not about building my kingdom. Jesus said that He came to do the will of the Father, and He preached: *"Repent for the kingdom of God is at hand."*

What is this kingdom? This is any realm where the King reigns. It is the total way of looking at life. This is revealed in Jesus, the King of Kings, in whom all the fullness of God dwells. The Kingdom is all comprehensive and all encompassing. Jesus came to reconcile all things to Himself (people, creation, differing spheres of society). The Kingdom sanctifies the common. It gives dignity to the things that the world says are menial. The

Meditations

cry of the Reformation was: *"Coram Deo,"* to live our life before the presence of God.
* The Kingdom is open to all.   John 3:16
* The Kingdom is now and not yet. Matthew 6:10
* The Kingdom is unshakeable.   Hebrews 12:28

Ask the Lord to cleanse your heart from any wrong motives about building your own kingdom. Invite Him to be number one in your life.

On Earth As It Is in Heaven

This is a cry to call forth that which is reality in heaven, so that it will also be made visible here on earth.

2 Corinthians 4:17-18 reminds us: *"Momentary, light affliction is producing for us an eternal weight of glory far beyond all comparison, while we look not at the things which are seen, but at the things which are not seen; for the things which are seen are temporal, but the things which are not seen are eternal"* (NASB).

Life is best lived in the light of eternity. There are many choices that can be made that will give a short-term result, but in light of eternity, they will seem inadequate. Ask God to help you to make the choices that will be a blessing in the long run. Jesus continually said that He only did what He saw the Father doing. In prayer, it is essential to ask the question: "Father, what is Your will, and what do You want to do in this situation?"

Give Us This Day Our Daily Bread

After whom we are talking to has been established, it is with utter confidence that we can come and make petition for our daily need of provision, pardon, and protection. These are our daily needs. In Matthew 6 we read how God cares for the lilies of the field and the birds of the air. How much more will He not care for us? He knows what we need and delights for us to ask Him to sustain us at the very deepest level of our existence. He not only provides for the physical needs that we have, but He *is* the Bread of Life for our spiritual nutrition.

Forgive Us Our Debts (moral debts/sins) As We Forgive Our Debtors

Forgiving and being forgiven are prerequisites for worship. If our lives are filled with broken relationships, we will find it hard to approach God. In fact, an unforgiving spirit can hinder healing. Forgiveness is a choice that we can make based on the fact that God, in Christ Jesus, has forgiven us all of our sins. It is, therefore, possible, through the power of the Holy Spirit, to forgive those who have wronged and/or hurt us.

When we look at the different miracles that Jesus did, we see that He addressed this issue of forgiveness in connection with healing and deliverance. God's grace is available and necessary in order to forgive, for this is not something that we can accomplish on our own. We forgive because He has forgiven us.

And Do Not Lead Us into Temptation, but Deliver Us From Evil (or the Evil One)

Understanding that we need God's help to live in the "minefield" of the present-day world is recognizing that we need God Himself. We can be tempted to compromise on moral and ethical issues. We can be tempted to give in to despair. We can be tempted to believe the lies that we are not loved, which the enemy of our soul tries to whisper in our ears. We can be tempted to believe the lies that God is not just, kind,

Meditations

good, righteous, loving, or faithful. We must do warfare, in our spirit, by applying what we read in Ephesians 6:10-17, allowing the truth of God's Word to be the anchor of our soul. Open your heart to the Holy Spirit, to bring a transformation to your thought life (see Philippians 4:8). Use the Word of God as a shield, when the fiery arrows of the enemy are aimed at you.

For Yours Is the Kingdom and the Power and the Glory Forever
Worship and adoration flow from our hearts when we have brought our burdens to a wonderful Father, who knows how to take care of His children. This gives us a sense of belonging, security, significance, and hope. He who comes to God must believe that He exists and is a Rewarder of those who seek Him.

To Ponder:
   * Take time to go back through this prayer and apply it to your situation in regard to seeking guidance in your life.
   * Dig deeper into the Scriptures about the names of the Lord. Ponder the significance that these names reveal to you about Him.
   * Are there people you need to extend forgiveness to?

To Pray:
Lord, thank You for Your help in receiving the guidance I need in life. Thank You for teaching me how to talk with You and listen to You in prayer. Expand my understanding of this wonderful privilege of what it means to live life before the audience of One.

Mirror, Mirror: A Reflected Life

THE WISDOM-FILLED LIFE (BASED ON PSALM 111:10)

**The fear of the LORD is the beginning of wisdom;
all who follow his precepts have good understanding.**

The Bible is very clear that in order to live life to the fullest, we need wisdom. The wisdom that is referred to encompasses all that is needed to live life skillfully. The book of Proverbs uses this key word 40 times to explain how to follow God's design for life and avoid moral pitfalls.

Many ask the question, "What does it mean to fear the Lord?" One of the best definitions I have come across for the fear of the Lord comes from a footnote in the New American Standard Bible: "A loving reverence for God that includes submission to His lordship and to the commands of His Word." In short, this means to shun evil, to do good, to trust and obey and allow Jesus to be number one in every area of life.

God is a holy God. It is His mercy and grace that we do not get what we deserve — namely, death. When we approach God, it must be on His terms, not ours. God cannot turn a blind eye to sin. Sin hinders our closeness with Him. It is destructive to us to live in rebellion against the Most High God. We are invited to repent of our sin. Psalm 130:3-4 says, *"If you, O LORD, kept a record of sins, O LORD, who could stand? But with you there is forgiveness; therefore you are feared."* This means a one-hundred-and-eighty-degree turn-around from the direction we have been going. It is not enough to confess, weep, and have remorse for what we have done. God is looking for genuine repentance.

Meditations

When we confess, we agree with God about what He says about sin and that what we have done *is* sin. Repentance is the choice to turn away from sin and walk by faith.

What am I continually speaking over my life? Matthew 12:34 tells us, *"For out of the overflow of the heart the mouth speaks."* Is what I speak in agreement with what God's Word declares?

Many times we are challenged in life to be more impressed with what people say about us than what God says about us. Having the fear of the Lord is the only way to be released from the fear of man. *"Fear of man will prove to be a snare"* (Proverbs 29:25).

The Bible teaches us that there are many blessings, as a reward for those who walk in the fear of the Lord. This inheritance of blessing is also meant for the generations that will come after us.

Psalm 115:13-14—*He will bless those who fear the Lord—small and great alike. May the Lord make you increase, both you and your children.*

Deuteronomy 5:29—*Oh, that their hearts would be inclined to fear me and keep all my commands always, so that it might go well with them and their children forever!*

Proverbs 14:26-27—*He who fears the Lord has a secure fortress, and for his children it will be a refuge. The fear of the Lord is a fountain of life, turning a man from the snares of death.*

To Ponder:
* Take time to reflect on what the word *wisdom* means. It means skill in living. Are there areas where you need more of this "skill"?

Mirror, Mirror: A Reflected Life

* What do you keep speaking over your life? Proverbs 18:21 shows us that *"death and life are in the power of the tongue"* (KJV). Maybe it is time to change your "language."
* Look up some of the blessings that the Lord promises to those who fear Him. Use them as a prayer of blessing.

To Pray:

Lord, thank You for teaching me how to live skillfully. Show me how to apply this to every area of my life. Life with You brings such great joy.

Part IV

Reflections

The following reflections are based on a variety of scripture passages and flowed from a time of reading the Word, reflecting on it, and then writing down what I saw in what I had just read.

Reflections

REFLECTIONS ON PSALM 23

The Lord is my shepherd, I shall not be in want.
He makes me lie down in green pastures,
he leads me beside quiet waters,
he restores my soul.
He guides me in paths of righteousness
for his name's sake.
Even though I walk
through the valley of the shadow of death,
I will fear no evil,
for you are with me;
your rod and your staff,
they comfort me.

You prepare a table before me
in the presence of my enemies.
You anoint my head with oil;
my cup overflows.
Surely goodness and love will follow me
all the days of my life,
and I will dwell in the house of the Lord
forever.

Your Lordship shepherds me.
Your care sustains me.
Your love enthralls me.
Your rule establishes me.
Your strength secures me.
Your power protects me.
Your presence satisfies me.

Mirror, Mirror: A Reflected Life

You have a place of:
 rest,
 refreshment,
 retreat,
 renewal and
 restoration for me.
Your guidance opens the:
 right doors,
 right paths,
 right relationships for me.
The journey may be over rugged terrain,
 along treacherous precipices,
 through deep valleys, for my soul.
But with You as my Guide,
 I need not entertain my worst fears of:
 separation,
 abandonment,
 powerlessness,
 worthlessness.
Your hand gently leads with firmness,
 yet so tenderly that my heart
 can only know acceptance.
You lavish me with a banquet for my soul.
All that has tripped me up in the past
 need not continue to triumph over me.
The abundance of Your presence
 causes my heart to sing with joy,
 knowing that I am not alone, but belong.

Reflections

REFLECTIONS ON HABAKKUK 3:17-19

Though the fig tree does not bud and there are no grapes on the vines,
though the olive crop fails and the fields produce no food,
though there are no sheep in the pen and no cattle in the stalls,
yet I will rejoice in the LORD,
I will be joyful in God my Savior.
The Sovereign LORD is my strength;
he makes my feet like the feet of a deer,
he enables me to go on the heights.

Though the stock market plummets,
  and the inventory shrinks,
  despite the barren cupboards,
  and depleted buying power,
You teach me the secret of peace
  in the midst of the storm.
As I lift my heart in jubilation,
  at Your sustaining presence,
You show me the path less travelled,
  that only those who trust can see.
My feet will walk
  with steadfast confidence.

Mirror, Mirror: A Reflected Life
Reflections on Psalm 42

As the deer pants for streams of water, so my soul pants for you, O God. My soul thirsts for God, for the living God.

Where can I go and meet with God? My tears have been my food day and night, while men say to me all day long, "Where is your God?" These things I remember as I pour out my soul: how I used to go with the multitude, leading the procession to the house of God, with shouts of joy and thanksgiving among the festive throng.

Why are you downcast, O my soul? Why so disturbed within me? Put your hope in God, for I will yet praise him, my Savior and my God. My soul is downcast within me; therefore I will remember you from the land of the Jordan, the heights of Hermon — from Mount Mizar.

Deep calls to deep in the roar of your waterfalls; all your waves and breakers have swept over me. By day the Lord directs his love, at night his song is with me — a prayer to the God of my life.

I say to God my Rock, "Why have you forgotten me? Why must I go about mourning, oppressed by the enemy?" My bones suffer mortal agony as my foes taunt me, saying to me all day long, "Where is your God?"

Why are you downcast, O my soul? Why so disturbed within me? Put your hope in God, for I will yet praise him, my Savior and my God.

Reflections

Longing is transformed into loving
  when I turn my heart toward You.
My soul is parched and thirsty;
  I turn my heart toward You.
Agony of spirit has been my companion,
  yet, I turn my heart toward You.
Memories of past accomplishments
  intensify my yearning
  to turn my heart toward You.
Despair will not triumph over me
  when I turn my heart toward You.
My heart is filled with homesick longing;
  despite this, I turn my heart toward You.
You surprise me with Your love and kindness,
  as I turn my heart toward You.
Your songs greet me on my pillow,
  if I turn my heart toward You.
Your melody unlocks my harmony
  each time I turn my heart toward You.
Defeat seems imminent,
  badgered with shouts,
  "Why turn your heart toward Him?"
Yet my song will rise.
My life will radiate the confidence I've found,
  by turning my heart toward You.

Mirror, Mirror: A Reflected Life

REFLECTIONS ON PSALM 46

*God is our refuge and strength,
A very present help in trouble.
Therefore we will not fear, though the earth should change
And though the mountains slip into the heart of the sea;
Though its waters roar and foam,
Though the mountains quake at its swelling pride.*

*There is a river whose streams make glad the city of God, The holy dwelling places of the Most High.
God is in the midst of her, she will not be moved;
God will help her when morning dawns.
The nations made an uproar, the kingdoms tottered;
He raised His voice, the earth melted.
The LORD of hosts is with us;
The God of Jacob is our stronghold.*

*Come, behold the works of the LORD,
Who has wrought desolations in the earth.
He makes wars to cease to the end of the earth;
He breaks the bow and cuts the spear in two,
He burns the chariots with fire.
"Cease striving and know that I am God;
I will be exalted among the nations, I will be exalted in the earth."
The LORD of hosts is with us;
The God of Jacob is our stronghold.* (NASB)

Troubled times bring our fears to the surface.
In the midst of the shaking, trembling, quaking of our foundations,

Reflections

God reveals:
His refuge,
His strength,
His help.
The violence of the crumbling world —
be it relational, economical, or physical,
(all things that have held our fascination,
anchored our determination,
underpinned our resolutions),
may quiver, flutter, vibrate, or rock our existence.
But His presence
tranquillizes,
equalizes,
stabilizes our fears.
Refreshment is available from the river that
flows from the Father's heart.
Gladness is poured forth,
which lifts our spirits to know that we need not be moved.
Meditate and see what He has done.
The violence, anger, hostility of the troubled world,
whose pride is set to bring destruction,
is no match for Him, who calms
the storms and rushing tides with just one word.
The arsenal of war poses no threat
to those who have learned to
wait,
cease striving,
relax, and know that He is God.
He has no equal.
All authority, might, power, dominion, radiance, glory
belong to Him.
Because He is, we are.

Mirror, Mirror: A Reflected Life
REFLECTIONS ON PSALM 91

He who dwells in the shelter of the Most High will rest in the shadow of the Almighty. I will say of the LORD, "He is my refuge and my fortress, my God, in whom I trust."

Surely he will save you from the fowler's snare and from the deadly pestilence. He will cover you with his feathers, and under his wings you will find refuge; his faithfulness will be your shield and rampart.

You will not fear the terror by night, nor the arrow that flies by day, nor the pestilence that stalks in the darkness, nor the plague that destroys at midday. A thousand may fall at your side, ten thousand at your right hand, but it will not come near you.

You will only observe with your eyes and see the punishment of the wicked. If you make the Most High your dwelling — even the LORD, who is my refuge — then no harm will befall you, no disaster will come near your tent.

For he will command his angels concerning you to guard you in all your ways; they will lift you up in their hands, so that you will not strike your foot against a stone. You will tread upon the lion and the cobra; you will trample the great lion and serpent.

"Because he loves me," says the Lord, "I will rescue him; I will protect him, for he acknowledges my name. He will call upon me, and I will answer him; I will be with him in trouble, I will deliver him and honor him. With long life will I satisfy him and show him my salvation.'

Reflections

Lord, being under Your shadow protects me from the burning sun and gives shade to receive Your cool refreshing presence.

Abiding in You is being at home with You. Being known and knowing gives me shelter from the trials of life.

It is a declaration from my lips that You provide the serenity and security that I need.

I can only jump up and hug You, because I KNOW You are as good as Your word.

Deadly traps surround me, both while sleeping and awake, yet I fear no harm because You cover me.

Your angelic host is mobilized as agents of this protective presence.

I need not face calamity with trepidation or dread, as You are always there when I put my trust in You.

You respond to my heart adoration.

Your love awakens my heart of love toward You.

You invite me to know You by Your true name.

You will always be:

IMMANUEL:	God with us;
EL SHADDAI:	The All-Sufficient One;
JEHOVAH SHALOM:	The Lord of Peace.

You unravel "trouble" to reveal the amazing tapestry of honor, blessing, anointing, and help, which You have provided every day of this journey.

Mirror, Mirror: A Reflected Life
Reflections on Isaiah 40:27-31

Why do you say, O Jacob, and complain, O Israel, "My way is hidden from the LORD; my cause is disregarded by my God?" Do you not know? Have you not heard? The LORD is the everlasting God, the Creator of the ends of the earth. He will not grow tired or weary, and his understanding no one can fathom. He gives strength to the weary and increases the power of the weak.

Even youths grow tired and weary, and young men stumble and fall; but those who hope in the LORD will renew their strength.

They will soar on wings like eagles; they will run and not grow weary, they will walk and not be faint.

Lord, there are moments when it seems like my way is hidden from Your sight, that the justice I think I deserve eludes me.

Yet, You invite me to consider Your grandeur, wisdom, and strength, instead of pondering the whys, hows and whens.

Your presence strengthens, empowers, and invigorates.

Those who recognize that their own resources are insufficient, inadequate and limited are given the key to release. It is in the waiting: expectantly, consciously, purposefully putting my full trust in You, the I AM, the Ancient of Days, Elohim.

Your enabling power and presence will make me to soar, renewed, revived and refreshed.

There are still more laps to the race that is before me.

Give me, Lord, the grace to reach the finish line.

Reflections

REFLECTIONS ON PSALM 100

Shout for joy to the LORD, all the earth.
Worship the LORD with gladness; come before him with joyful songs.
Know that the LORD is God.
It is he who made us, and we are his;
We are his people, the sheep of his pasture.
Enter his gates with thanksgiving and his courts with praise; give thanks to him and praise his name.
For the LORD is good and his love endures for ever; his faithfulness continues through all generations.

Lord, Your character is guarantor for Your promises.
The earth is summed to attention.
Joy and gladness roll over my lips, as I rehearse who it is that has formed me.
Your care, provision, and nurture are so specific to each human heart.
You have a place of retreat, refreshment, and renewal that fit my sheep-like needs.
The gateway to Your fold is through the disciplines of gratitude and praise.
Your name is to be praised above all else.
Your goodness knows no end.
Your love knows no end.
Your kindness knows no end.
Your faithfulness knows no end.
Each generation will rise up to declare Your glory, dignity, and might to the next.

Mirror, Mirror: A Reflected Life

Reflections on Psalm 84

*How lovely are Your dwelling places,
O Lord of hosts!
My soul longed and even yearned for the courts
of the Lord;
My heart and my flesh sing for joy to the living God.
The bird also has found a house,
And the swallow a nest for herself, where she may
lay her young,
Even Your altars, O Lord of hosts,
My King and my God.
How blessed are those who dwell in Your house!
They are ever praising You.*

*How blessed is the man whose strength is in You,
In whose heart are the highways to Zion!
Passing through the valley of Baca* [weeping] *they
make it a spring;
The early rain also covers it with blessings.
They go from strength to strength,
Every one of them appears before God in Zion.*

*O Lord God of hosts, hear my prayer;
Give ear, O God of Jacob!
Behold our shield, O God,
And look upon the face of Your anointed.
For a day in Your courts is better than a thousand
outside.
I would rather stand at the threshold of the house
of my God
Than dwell in the tents of wickedness.*

Reflections

*For the L*ORD *God is a sun and shield;*
*The L*ORD *gives grace and glory;*
No good thing does He withhold from those who walk uprightly.
*O L*ORD *of hosts,*
How blessed is the man who trusts in You! (NASB)

O Lord Almighty, blessed is the man who trusts in You.
Your home is so inviting.
My heart eagerly looks for the opportunity to just be with You.
I have had a foretaste of the splendor of Your presence.
I am spoiled for anything else.
Something about being with You releases a song within my being that cannot be contained.
It unlocks resources I never thought could be available, to scale the peaks of life or to journey through the barren moments, when all fruitfulness seems but a distant memory.
Something about being with You energizes, invigorates, empowers, and enthralls me to be all that You had in mind for me to become.
You listen and hear the prayers tumbling over my lips.
All I can say is that I want to be with You.
You are the Warmth on my path, my Protector on the way.
You abundantly pour out Your generous grace, which enables me to declare my trust, even when answers are yet to come.

Mirror, Mirror: A Reflected Life

REFLECTIONS ON PSALM 1

Blessed is the man
 who does not walk in the counsel of the wicked,
 or stand in the way of sinners,
 or sit in the seat of mockers.
But his delight is in the law of the Lord,
 and on his law he meditates day and night.
He is like a tree planted by streams of water,
  which yields its fruit in season
 and whose leaf does not wither.
Whatever he does prospers.

Not so the wicked!
They are like chaff
 that the wind blows away.
Therefore the wicked will not stand in the judgment,
 nor sinners in the assembly of the righteous.

For the Lord watches over the way of the righteous,
 but the way of the wicked will perish.

Happiness awaits those who choose wisely where they walk,
  not positioning themselves with those who despise Your name,
 nor subtly settling for defiance against Your laws.
Pure joy awaits those who have learned to
 ponder, think, reflect on Your words of truth.
Life awaits those who have learned to draw from the Source.
They are compared to a tree with deep roots,
 drawing life from a place not visible to the human eye.
Happiness, joy, and life produce fruit,
 abundance for each season of life.

Reflections

REFLECTIONS ON ISAIAH 9:2 AND 6

The people walking in darkness
have seen a great light;
on those living in the land of the
shadow of death a light has dawned.
For to us a child is born,
to us a son is given,
and the government will be on his shoulders.
And he will be called
Wonderful Counselor, Mighty God,
Everlasting Father, Prince of Peace.

A child will be given, so small, helpless, fragile, whose destiny will be to shatter the chains of darkness, to rule with justice and grace, to establish the reign of heaven on earth. Would we recognize, in that tiny face, the imprint of His Father? Would we really grasp what Majesty had chosen for humanity?

The people are walking in darkness, searching, groping, stumbling, waiting for the light, which would illuminate and dispel the weight of walking alone.

A faint cry, at birth, echoes through eternity. His mission, commission, submission was to bring Life, life as we have never known it before. Free from the stain of rebellion and self, from worshiping the created instead of the Creator.

What is in a name? Who will our heart cry out to when the keys to life have been lost?

Wonderful Counselor: one filled with wisdom to split the atom, resolve life's mega-questions, showing the way to love.

Mirror, Mirror: A Reflected Life

Mighty God: unexcelled in strength, counting the stars, while spinning galaxies into eternity, yet close enough to carry each life near to His heart.

Eternal Father: His life brings me truly home, where I am loved without performing, encouraged without strings attached, admonished and blessed, just because I am. The Master Designer, who longs for me to call him Daddy, writes my value and worth on each cell.

Prince of Peace: Defeat is not a word in His vocabulary. His Kingdom bestows wellness, wholeness, wellbeing, and life to each citizen. Just one word is enough to calm the raging sea, one prayer enough to turn the water into wine, one blessing enough to take the loaves and feed the multitude, one life enough, given on a cross in exchange for freedom for humanity — until the end of time.

Reflections

REFLECTIONS ON ISAIAH 61:1-3

The Spirit of the Sovereign LORD is on me,
  because the LORD has anointed me to preach
  good news to the poor.
He has sent me to bind up the brokenhearted,
  to proclaim freedom for the captives
  and release from darkness for the prisoners,
to proclaim the year of the LORD's favor
  and the day of vengeance of our God,
to comfort all who mourn,
  and provide for those who grieve in Zion —
to bestow on them a crown of beauty
  instead of ashes,
the oil of gladness
  instead of mourning,
and a garment of praise
  instead of a spirit of despair.
They will be called oaks of righteousness,
  a planting of the Lord
  for the display of his splendor.

From earth's foundation, the message was prepared:
Your life would be given, redemption's song would be sung,
  the Good News of heaven invading earth,
  the Kingdom of light, triumphant over the gates of hell.
All who are afflicted, whose heart has been broken,
  await Your healing word.
Your restoring embrace sets the captive free.
No prison door can withstand Your call to freedom.

Mirror, Mirror: A Reflected Life

Captivity and imprisonment do not have the last word
  when Your sacrifice is embraced.
So many mourn.
There are so many broken dreams.
The streets are filled with countless shattered lives.
But Your promise is to comfort *all* who mourn.
Your broad shoulders absorb the deep wailing and weeping
  of a world that's lost its way.
You extend a hand, but only an empty one can receive Yours.
You take the ashes of each life and give beauty instead,
  a beauty based on the reality of being loved.
Your smile of acceptance thrills each heart,
  enabling the rise from despondency,
  to become what You intended.
You bathe each one in the oil of Your presence,
  gladness, and joy.
You celebrate life and lift the shroud of mourning.
The only appropriate response,
  as the bronze doors swing open,
  the heavy chains of bondage fall off,
  is celebration of life as it was intended to be.
Exquisite robes of praise and worship clothe
  the naked and shamed.
The fainting spirit is dispelled when the crescendo
  of heaven is sung.
The high praises of our God on each lip
  bring light to even the darkest regions of the soul.

Reflections

REFLECTIONS ON MICAH 6:8

He has showed you, O man, what is good.
And what does the LORD require of you?
To act justly and to love mercy
and to walk humbly with your God.

We have not been left without instructions.
The One whose fingerprint we contain
  has shared what brings Him pleasure.
Justice is His nature, character, and song.
He is fairness, equality, honor, dignity, and honesty.
Nothing about Him is dark or manipulative.
His children are called to walk in His footsteps.
Kindness reflects His heart.
It draws us to His redeeming love.
As we are loved, we learn to love.
As His kindness penetrates our defenses,
  it ignites a response of like kind.
Humility will shatter the
  proud chains of bondage,
  as it acknowledges that there is only One
  who deserves all the praise,
  only One who can unlock the wellspring of life,
   only One who has wisdom, knowledge, and discernment.
Walking with Him enables us to become like Him.
His whisper of hope resonates,
  calling us to follow.

Mirror, Mirror: A Reflected Life

REFLECTIONS ON PSALM 103:1-5

Praise the L<small>ORD</small>, O my soul;
  all my inmost being, praise his holy name.
Praise the L<small>ORD</small>, O my soul,
  and forget not all his benefits —
who forgives all your sins
  and heals all your diseases,
who redeems your life from the pit
  and crowns you with love and compassion,
who satisfies your desires with good things,
  so that your youth is renewed like the eagle's.

Awake, my soul, to sing of Your grace.
Awake, my soul, to sing of Your glory.
Awake, my soul, to sing of Your goodness.
It is never-ending, all-encompassing, enduring, eternal.
Awake, my soul, to meditate on Your pardon.
Awake, my soul, to ponder on Your provision.
Awake, my soul, to think on Your protection.
It is never-ending, all-encompassing, enduring, eternal.
Awake, my soul, to receive Your healing.
Awake, my soul, to embrace Your redemption.
Awake, my soul, to believe Your Word.
It is never-ending, all-encompassing, enduring, eternal.
You crown my life with loving-kindness.
You crown my life with beauty.
You crown my life with compassion.
You alone satisfy.
You alone renew.
You alone are my heart's desire.

Reflections

REFLECTIONS ON JOHN 15:11

I have told you this so that my joy may be in you and my joy may be complete.

Joy: a sneak preview of Heaven

Your thunderous laughter of delight fills heaven's glory.
Your joy is a wellspring, flooding my soul with hope.
Your joy will be my joy.
This joy is based on integrity.
Your character backs up Your promise.
This joy reveals my identity.
My value is anchored in Your sacrifice.
This joy unlocks the itinerary.
It is now and not yet, but is to come.

Mirror, Mirror: A Reflected Life
REFLECTIONS ON PSALM 27:1-4

The LORD is my light and my salvation —
  whom shall I fear?
The LORD is the stronghold of my life —
  of whom shall I be afraid?
When evil men advance against me
  to devour my flesh,
when my enemies and my foes attack me,
  they will stumble and fall.
Though an army besiege me,
  my heart will not fear;
though war break out against me,
  even then will I be confident.

One thing I ask of the LORD,
  this is what I seek:
that I may dwell in the house of the LORD
  all the days of my life,
to gaze upon the beauty of the LORD
  and to seek him in his temple.

You illuminate my darkness.
Your gaze pierces every corner.
Your gift gives freedom instead of chains.
With You at my side,
  You defend.
Your defense,
  Your deliverance is complete.
I need not dread the adversarial foes.
They are cut off; their pursuit nullified.
My enemies are not pacified, but defeated.

Reflections

My confidence is based on
  the One who conquered the grave.
Therefore my heart will not shudder,
  but hope in the day of distress.
My heart is filled with homesick longing,
  as I seek to gaze in Your face.
A wellspring of delight is released into my life.

Mirror, Mirror: A Reflected Life
REFLECTIONS ON MATTHEW 28:18-20

Then Jesus came to them and said, "All authority in heaven and on earth has been given to me. Therefore go and make disciples of all nations, baptizing them in the name of the Father and of the Son and of the Holy Spirit, and teaching them to obey everything I have commanded you. And surely I am with you always, to the very end of the age."

He was authorized by the King of heaven Himself.
Conquering the grave gave Him the right to declare
　His complete authority over the visible and invisible.
There is no throne of power which exceeds His domain,
　no court jurisdiction which surpasses His verdict.
His word is established before the beginning of time
　and will know no end.
He did not usurp this authority,
　but was given it by the Father.
From a complete place of security, He commands us to go.
The ticket is paid, the itinerary laid out,
　the message prepared.
Transformation is at the heart of the command,
　affecting systems, policies, legislatures that govern
　and guide nations, calling each to respond
　to the One who has the keys of life and death in His hands,
　immersing each believer in the water of cleansing,
　laying aside the old,
　embracing and welcoming the new.
Education is necessary,

Reflections

as we don't implicitly know
the ways of the Kingdom.
Our language doesn't include the vocabulary of the King.
Allegiance, obedience and humble submission
to a new way of life
come from a deep encounter with Life itself.
Oh, His promise breaks the sound barrier:
"I am with you always" echoes into each lonely heart.
The core of separation and isolation is disbanded
when this union is availed of.
This reality shatters the lies of insecurity, insignificance,
and the inability to embrace life.
There will never be a moment that He is not there.

Mirror, Mirror: A Reflected Life

REFLECTIONS ON ZEPHANIAH 3:14-17

Sing, O Daughter of Zion;
  shout aloud, O Israel!
Be glad and rejoice with all your heart,
  O Daughter of Jerusalem!
The LORD has taken away your punishment,
  he has turned back your enemy.
The LORD, the King of Israel, is with you;
  never again will you fear any harm.
On that day they will say to Jerusalem,
  "Do not fear, O Zion;
  do not let your hands hang limp.
The LORD your God is with you,
  he is mighty to save.
He will take great delight in you,
  he will quiet you with his love,
  he will rejoice over you with singing."

Joy rings forth when the prison doors are opened.
Judgment is absorbed into the nail-pierced hands.
Fear of enemy attack, impending doom,
  trepidation, and paralysis must flee
  at the presence of the King.
His arrival marks victory.
His comfort brings rest.
His love begets love.
His song pierces the heart with joy.

Reflections

REFLECTIONS ON HEBREWS 12:1-3

Therefore, since we are surrounded by such a great cloud of witnesses, let us throw off everything that hinders and the sin that so easily entangles, and let us run with perseverance the race marked out for us. Let us fix our eyes on Jesus, the author and perfector of our faith, who for the joy set before him endured the cross, scorning its shame, and sat down at the right hand of the throne of God. Consider him who endured such opposition from sinful men, so that you will not grow weary and lose heart.

The bleachers are filled with expectant faces.
The spectators believe in us,
  know we can do it,
  know who trained us.
Lay aside the entanglements.
The course has been set when our focus is fixed on Him.
He paved the way through His own training and sacrifice.
He asks only that which He has done Himself.
He saw us as His crown, joy, reward,
  while He walked the lonely road,
  hung on a tree,
  and paid the ultimate price.
He could have escaped the shame and humiliation,
  but, instead, He endured,
 taking that which disqualified me upon Himself.
Now I can run with my face lifted up,
  bathed in the sunshine of His presence,
  hearing only His cheer.

Mirror, Mirror: A Reflected Life

Reflections on Psalm 96:1-3

Sing to the LORD a new song;
  sing to the LORD, all the earth.
Sing to the LORD, praise his name;
  proclaim his salvation day after day.
Declare his glory among the nations,
  his marvelous deeds among all peoples.

The unsung song,
  the seed of redemption,
  so small, so fragile,
  unseen to the naked eye,
  when planted in hearts
  open to hear,
  of One whose image
  is not captured in bronze or flare,
  releases the song
  that was sung
  from the beginning of time.
"Worthy are You,
  our Lord and our God,
  to receive glory, honor, power.
For You created all things
  and because of Your will,
    they existed and were created."
They, who futilely tried
  to find the One
  whose song they were intended to sing,
  instead, made rhythms and rhymes,
  to wood and clay,
  using the created
  to approach Him who existed before time began.

Reflections

All it takes is one small seed,
  planted in any human heart,
  to unlock eternity placed there
  from the beginning of time.
The floodgates of sin and shame
  must openly submit to the One
  whose bruises and stripes
  and nail-pierced hands
  carried the blame.
These vibrant tunes will resonate
  across each generation,
  "From every tribe, tongue, people, and nation.
For He has made them to be a kingdom
  and priest to our God
  and they will reign upon the earth."

Mirror, Mirror: A Reflected Life
Reflections on John 3:16

For God so loved the world that he gave his one and only Son, that whoever believes in him shall not perish but have eternal life.

For God so loved the world,
  this tattered orb,
  swirling around in time and space,
  oblivious to the Great Design,
  whose inhabitants war and make war,
  consuming His love without regard,
  enslaving its children
  in prisons of consumption,
  wondering why their choices
  have taken them so far away from home.

For God so loved this world,
  which He crafted with such delight,
  spinning the stars out into galaxies,
  giving the Son to warm each cold heart.
His fingerprint is reflected in a multitude
  of variations in color, language, custom,
  and song.

For God so loved this world,
  which discards its unborn,
  eliminates its elderly,
  marginalizes its mentally challenged,
  unable to acknowledge that He does care
  for that which seemingly has no ability
  to repay or consume.

Reflections

For God so loved this world
  that He devised a plan.
He would shoulder the blame,
  fulfilling the criteria
  of carrying the shame.
It cost Him His Son,
  His pure delight,
  who'd accompanied Him
  from before time began.
He walked the road of the cross,
  submitting to His own laws of gravity,
  covered with humility,
  to seal our destiny.
The exchange is so unequal,
  the invitation so lavish.
I give Him my death;
  He gives me His life.
His tears, as an abandoned Father moves Him to say,
  "I have loved you
  with an everlasting love
  which knows no end."

Postscript

Life is filled with countless "mirrors" that project a reflection, which can be either very accurate or extremely distorted. During childhood, subtle choices are made as to which of these projections we will believe and follow. The pages you have just read have been written as a story of redemption in the midst of wrong and distorted choices that were made in my own life. I am grateful for my birth family and the choices they made to try to be the best "mirrors" they knew how to be for me, despite the cracks and broken pieces which distorted some of the reflection.

Above all, my heart is filled with deep gratitude to the Lord, for His persistence in my life, not only to help me change the "mirrors" I looked to for my anchor, but also for how He has restored my vision, enabling me to see life and myself more clearly.

My first attempt at putting my thoughts down on paper came after the arrival of my first grandchild. As I looked into her tiny face, a desire began to grow in my heart to share with her the lessons I had learned, hopefully enabling her to avoid the pitfalls I had encountered along my journey in life.

Over the years, I had shared various stories with my children, but had not, as yet, compiled them in such a way as to pass them on to the next generation.

Mirror, Mirror: A Reflected Life

Soul searching is never an easy process, nor are all of the things that surface intended to be shared. The events that have been shared here are intended to give a framework that would represent, in a very concise way, what God can do in a life to bring health and wholeness to the inner person.

This book is, thus, a dedication to the generations who will follow me. My prayer is that this will form a legacy of life for them to draw from and which, in turn, will point them to the Well-Spring of all life, Jesus Himself.

www.ingramcontent.com/pod-product-compliance
Lightning Source LLC
LaVergne TN
LVHW051603070426
835507LV00021B/2744